ORDINARY TIME

ALSO BY SARAH M. WELLS

Pruning Burning Bushes

Between the Heron and the Moss

American Honey: A Field Guide to Resisting Temptation

The Family Bible Devotional: Stories from the Bible to Help Kids and Parents Engage and Love Scripture

The Family Bible Devotional Vol. 2: Stories from the Gospels to Help Kids and Parents Love God and Love Others

Ordinary Time

Meditations from the In-Between

by SARAH M. WELLS

RESOURCE *Publications* • Eugene, Oregon

ORDINARY TIME
Meditations from the In-Between

Copyright © 2024 Sarah M. Wells. All rights reserved. Except for brief quotations in critical publications or reviews, no part of this book may be reproduced in any manner without prior written permission from the publisher. Write: Permissions, Wipf and Stock Publishers, 199 W. 8th Ave., Suite 3, Eugene, OR 97401.

Resource Publications
An Imprint of Wipf and Stock Publishers
199 W. 8th Ave., Suite 3
Eugene, OR 97401

www.wipfandstock.com

PAPERBACK ISBN: 979-8-3852-1022-0
HARDCOVER ISBN: 979-8-3852-1023-7
EBOOK ISBN: 979-8-3852-1024-4
04/01/24

Unless otherwise indicated, all Scripture quotations are taken from the (NASB®) New American Standard Bible®, Copyright © 1960, 1971, 1977, 1995, 2020 by The Lockman Foundation. Used by permission. All rights reserved. lockman.org

Scripture quotations marked (KJV) are taken from The Authorized (King James) Version. Rights in the Authorized Version in the United Kingdom are vested in the Crown. Reproduced by permission of the Crown's patentee, Cambridge University Press.

Scripture quotations marked (NRSV) are taken from the New Revised Standard Version Bible: Anglicized Edition, copyright © 1989, 1995 National Council of the Churches of Christ in the United States of America. Used by permission. All rights reserved worldwide.

Scripture quotations marked (NIV) are taken from the Holy Bible, New International Version®, NIV®. Copyright © 1973, 1978, 1984, 2011 by Biblica, Inc.™ Used by permission of Zondervan. All rights reserved worldwide. www.zondervan.com The "NIV" and "New International Version" are trademarks registered in the United States Patent and Trademark Office by Biblica, Inc.™

*for Elvis Elijah Davis Wells
and for Roseann Fugman*

*Creation is the language of God,
Time is His song,
and things of space
the consonants in the song.
To sanctify time
is to sing the vowels in unison with Him.*

ABRAHAM JOSHUA HESCHEL, THE SABBATH

Contents

Acknowledgements | ix

Introduction | xi

Miles to Go Before I Sleep | 1

Soup: A History | 8

The Body Is Not a Coffin | 16

Country Boys, City Boys | 29

Little Joys: Music | 40

Family Tradition | 42

The Empty Spaces | 50

Those Summers, These Days | 51

The Lord's Name | 63

Underwater | 69

15 | 76

Skipping Stones | 95

Little Joys: Neural Intimacy | 96

The Violence of the Given World | 98

Little Joys: The Woods | 105

Advent and Everything After | 107

Sabbath Afternoon | 116

Little Joys: Books | 118

Foxglove, Bee Balm | 120

Mothers' Top Dresser Drawers | 127

Ordinary Time | 129

Little Joys: Walkability | 135

The Things We've Lost and Where They're Found | 137

The Wonders of Massaman Curry | 140

Little Joys: Bodies That Can Heal | 146

The Resurrection Life | 148

Crickets | 153

What Did and Didn't Last | 159

Bibliography | 161

Acknowledgements

I AM grateful to the editors of the following journals where these essays, sometimes in earlier versions, first appeared:

Ascent, "Ordinary Time" and "Those Summers, These Days"
Awst Press, "The Lord's Name"
Brevity, "The Empty Spaces" (brevity blog) and "Mothers' Top Dresser Drawers"
God Hears Her, "The Resurrection Life"
Relief Journal, "Underwater"
River Teeth: A Journal of Nonfiction Narrative, "Country Boys, City Boys" and "Skipping Stones" (Beautiful Things series)
Rock & Sling, "The Wonders of Massaman Curry"
Terrain.org: A Journal of the Built + Natural Environments, "Foxglove, Bee Balm" and "The Violence of the Given World"
Tiferet Journal, "Miles to Go Before I Sleep"
Under the Gum Tree, "The Body Is Not a Coffin"

"Those Summers, These Days," "The Body Is Not a Coffin," and "Country Boys, City Boys" were listed as Notable Essays in *Best American Essays*.

"The Violence of the Given World" won the Terrain.org 9th Annual Nonfiction Contest and was nominated for inclusion in the Pushcart Prize Anthology.

"The Body Is Not a Coffin" was nominated for inclusion in the Pushcart Prize Anthology.

Acknowledgements

Grateful acknowledgement to the Ohio Arts Council for its support via the Individual Excellence Award.

All of these people and their wisdom, vulnerability, laughter, humility, and compassion have formed me. So really, this book is their fault.

Thank you, Brandon, for continuing to champion my work. You are my true companion, my best friend, and my favorite person. Thank you for helping me to see the sacred in these ordinary moments. *It is a good day.*

Lydia, Elvis, and Henry, you three make my life rich with love, joy (big and little), and laughter.

Thank you, parents: Mom, a million times thank you. I am so blessed to be your daughter. I love you and will always say so. Dad, every word I've ever written about you is rooted in love. Thank you. Gary and Rhonda, how wonderful it is to be friends with your in-laws. How blessed am I, even if I'm not blood! Thank you for your abundant love and encouragement.

Becca, Julie, Jewls, LeeAnn, Jillian, Kim, Jody, Maura, Lisa, Angie, Emily, Jen, Allison, Colleen, Karen, Stacey, Laura, Low E wives, and the Monday Ladies Tea Group . . . I am surrounded by strong, brilliant women, which I've decided is the best way to go through life. Thank you for your friendship.

Woodland Creatures, you know who you are. Thanks for making authentic spirituality a core value of the writing life.

Thank you, Ashland University family; I miss you crazy MFAers.

George and Janet, Bernie and Pidge, Tony, Miles, Nate, Bill, the folks at Park Street Brethren and 5 Stones, and the Brethren Coffee group, thank you for challenging me and loving me just as I am. Y'all are the body of Christ.

Introduction

I HAVE focused on what comes next for most of my life. *After I graduate high school, I will go to college. After I graduate college, I will get married. After I get married, I will have babies.* In linear time, there's a ladder to climb with specific goals on each rung. I am a keeper of lists, an annual resolution generator, and few things give me more pleasure than checkmarks next to line items on an agenda. *Yes! I did it! Now what?*

When you climb a ladder, you don't look at where you are. You look to see where you're heading. But sometimes the rungs of the ladder underneath you snap.

The marriage you hoped for falters. You miscarry the child you wanted. The parent you thought would live forever develops cancer. The job you dreamed of disappears. In these moments, ordinary time quickly transitions into extraordinary time.

For centuries, many in the church have followed what is known as the liturgical calendar—a calendar that exists outside of linear time. Its objective is to remember and celebrate the life of Jesus and the life of the church. For about six months of the year, followers of Jesus remember the hope and anticipation of a Savior (Advent), the incarnation of the Son of God (Christmas), the revelation of Jesus' earthly ministry (Epiphany), Jesus' wilderness journey (Lent), Jesus' death and Resurrection (Easter), and the gift of the Holy Spirit given in conjunction with Jesus' ascension (Pentecost).

The remainder of the year is called Ordinary Time. This season runs from about June to late November, when the church resumes its trek through the life and ministry of Jesus once more. Churches spend a lot of

Introduction

time and energy preparing for the bookends of birth (Christmas) and death (Easter) in the life of Jesus. Many a Nativity is stashed in church closets with boxes upon boxes of garlands and lights, waiting for Advent. Every sanctuary awaits the placement of palms, anticipating the triumphant King's arrival. Entire church staffs rally to celebrate these church holidays.

In contrast, Ordinary Time often feels like the time we need to just "get through" in order to reach the next landmark.

Even when we know it's coming and believe it is good—a birth, a marriage, a job change—whatever it is, it is new, it is surprising, and it is hard. "Hard" might be the undercurrent of the rest of the liturgical calendar. From birth to death to Resurrection, Jesus made all things new, and making all things new is complicated, challenging, and painful.

Early on in the global pandemic, I developed long COVID, and after a few months of mysterious symptoms and debilitating fatigue, I decided to resign from my position of leadership at a local marketing agency.

I didn't see this coming. Resignation was not in my ten-year plan. I was trucking along happily in ordinary time when the ladder gave out underneath me. The result of that resignation was far more of a blessing than I could have ever anticipated. In the last couple of years, the corporate ladder I was climbing got turned on its side. I'm using it now to dry my laundry. God has made ordinary time my priority.

I don't mean to say that I no longer do anything of substance. What I mean to say is that everything I do now feels substantive. The ordinary just felt mundane before, something to survive in order to get to the next great thing. But ordinary time is half of our cyclical lives, and I don't want to just get through half of my life. All of the space granted by ordinary time gives us room to grow. Ordinary time is the long pocket of time given to us for rest, for preparation, and for joy. It is—or it can be—a kind of constant Sabbath, the kind Hebrew scholar Abraham Joshua Heschel described as "a palace in time with a kingdom for all."[1]

If we do not step into ordinary time, we will spin from miracle to tragedy and back again in a constant frenzy, with no time to reflect, only time to react. The holiday season from October to January is a good example. We hurry up and put up the Halloween decorations and then hurry up to tear them down to hurry up and be thankful and then quickly store the turkey

---

1. Abraham Joshua Heschel, *The Sabbath: Its Meaning for Modern Man*, 21.

Introduction

platter to make room for the Advent wreath and a hundred other decorations to make ready for Christmas magic. This frenetic existence during the holidays and beyond—into our everyday lives—leads to burnout, spiritual fatigue or exhaustion, depression, and anxiety.

That is why ordinary time is a gift. When Jesus wasn't being born miraculously, healing the blind and diseased, leading a band of disoriented and well-meaning disciples, and raising the dead, He ate and slept. He prayed and learned. He worked alongside others. He rested. Between the seasons of great distress and blessing, Jesus had ordinary time to process and prepare. Between our own seasons of distress and blessing, we have ordinary time to process and prepare as well.

Several significant crises have shaped the last fifteen years of my life. A crisis by definition is a turning point, for better or for worse. One was the birth of my son, Elvis, who spent ten days in the NICU when he was first born. Another was the subject of my memoir, *American Honey*. My mom's kidney cancer diagnosis a decade ago and my own bout of chronic illness that began with the pandemic round out most of the more significant crises, with a few minor crises tacked on here and there. In between these landmark occasions in linear time, there have been long seasons of ordinary existence.

The extraordinary thing about time is that the events that happen in linear time are layered, like phyllo dough. What happened fifteen years ago didn't just happen and then evaporate; those momentous events ripple and wrinkle the sheet of events that follows, forever. Our seasons of crisis flavor our seasons of ordinary life. Whatever traumas or ecstasies we experience occur in an instant, but their impression on us shapes who we become and how we behave in every instant, forevermore.

The essays in *Ordinary Time* are celebrations of small joys and reflections on how some of the triggering events of my life have affected the ordinary life I live. Ordinary time hides the incarnate Christ in plain sight and then invites us on a treasure hunt. We look in all the obvious places—Christmas, Easter, Good Friday—only to discover that the flavor of Christ is here, there, and everywhere, infused in creation's every particle. There is so much to find here in ordinary time, so much to cherish, so much to learn. With any hope, the unveiling rawness of our traumas and ecstasies simultaneously unveils the beauty in sheer existence.

This is your invitation to step into my palace in time.

Miles to Go Before I Sleep

WE talk about growing old, my mom and I. We talk about the crankiness of some old people, the games they play, the things they say, the way they lay blame, the way they've changed. Tomorrow she will turn fifty-four. Together we plan to take my daughter to lunch and to see *My Big Fat Greek Wedding 2*. The first movie is one of our favorites; we quote it nearly weekly: "I peel the potatoes . . . OH, it's a CAAAAKE . . . Toula, when are you going to get married? You look so . . . old."

I have three children now, children who always measure up an age, almost-ten, almost-nine, almost-five—ever eager to be older. When my mom was my age, I was thirteen-going-on-fourteen, and all of my grandparents were alive. All of my grandmothers are still alive. All of my children's great-grandmothers are still alive.

My last living great-grandmother, Anna B. Lingro, stuck around until she was ninety-four. She died in April of 2002. *2002?!* Why did I think it was so much earlier? In my head I thought she had died in 1997, but it turns out she died much later. It was my grandpa who passed away in 1997. Grandpas shouldn't go before great-grandmas.

Last night, I dreamt I remembered at a conference that my oldest son Elvis was shot dead. A girl was talking about how *you can't know my grief* and I nodded and waited until she walked away because whose grief is impersonal, whose grief is common? No one's. No one knows the depths of your personal grief. In my dream, after she left I collapsed alone. *My son is dead, he's dead, shot dead.* I woke up dry sobbing, clutching my comforter.

He is not dead, he is not dead, he is not dead.

Ordinary Time

The church ladies we know in their seventies and eighties and nineties, and some into a full century, they smile and laugh and seem to keep on living. They aren't cranky, even though they've surely known grief. Mom's friends who live in Florida play golf in the morning and evening. "Can you imagine your grandma swinging a golf club?" Mom asks.

"Maybe Putt-Putt," I say back. Mom mimes what that might look like and we laugh, sad.

I was nineteen-going-on-twenty the spring my great-grandma died, breaking up with boys every two weeks as soon as I knew they weren't the One. In a few months, I'd meet my future husband, the future father of my children. They would have some memory of all of their grandparents and four of their great-grandmothers.

My sons talk about guns and knives and killing things, all the time. They play soldiers and Star Wars and make dozens of virtual enemies on Disney Infinity just so they can kill them. Elvis jumps up and down as it happens, as they attack. The memory space bar on the right of the screen reaches red and I shout over the glee, "Stop making so many enemies!"

Elvis almost died when he was born. He couldn't suck in enough air unless he screamed, diagnosed with respiratory distress syndrome even though he was considered full-term. RDS babies can't make enough surfactant. Their lungs collapse, cutting off oxygen to the rest of the body's organs. They hooked him up to many machines in the Akron Children's Hospital NICU, and for ten days he stayed.

"I would shoot him in the face!" I hear from the back seat.

I sigh, "Don't talk like that."

"Mom, we're talking about zombies," they say. Obviously, they are talking about zombies.

"What is a zombie?" I ask Google. Google says it's a corpse revived by witchcraft, a dead thing brought back to a state of undead.

Toula's aunt sits down with Toula's future in-laws in *My Big Fat Greek Wedding*. "Now you are family," she says. "Okay. All my life . . . I had a lump at the back of my neck. Right here. Always a lump. Then I started menopause, and the lump got bigger. From the hormones, it started to grow. So, I go to the doctor, and he did the . . . the bios . . . the . . . the bubopsy. Inside the lump, he found teeth . . . and a spinal cord. Yes, inside the lump . . . was my twin."

Because she's young and healthy, my mom and I are often mistaken for sisters. After her biopsy, the nurses remark on our resemblance. The doctor who performed the procedure was 90% sure the growth was renal cell carcinoma. She had been stage I, until traces of that variety of cancer popped up in lymph nodes in her lungs. Popped up. That makes it sound better, doesn't it? Like maybe they could be popped back down, like a soap bubble blown from the edge of a wand.

What is it with the lungs, here? I can't even catch my breath. Stage IV kidney cancer. Stage IV kidney cancer. When a friend complains, when the work schedule changes, when someone sends a rant through social media or pouts over a decision about wallpaper, *it doesn't matter, my mom has cancer. It doesn't matter, my mom has cancer.* Breathe in. Breathe out. Breathe in. Breathe out.

"Then the Lord God formed man of dust from the ground, and breathed into his nostrils the breath of life; and man became a living being."[1]

Kidney cancer is unpredictable—you could have six to nine months or live as long as a decade. Because she's young and healthy, she has a choice—try Interleukin-2, the only chance for a cure, or succumb to the other, more mild, treatments. Treatments to prolong life. Treatments to delay death.

---

1. Gen 2:7.

Ordinary Time

I tell Elvis he can't play on the PlayStation anymore tonight. There have been too many enemies created, too many outbursts from his younger brother, whining, "Stop killing me!" too many sorrows, and I am tired of it all. "If you don't get off of there right now you won't play again tomorrow!" He scurries through the buttons to the power-down option and then collapses, moaning, on the floor. I am the worst. Mom. Ever.

Grief is personal.

What are the chances for cure? I ask Google. Interleukin-2 (IL-2) has a 5 percent success rate, says Google. Thirty-five percent of patients see some tumor shrinkage or stoppage and go for a long time without any growth. And 60 percent see no change at all.

Besides Star Wars, and Legos, and Lego Star Wars, and playing Star Wars on the PS4, Elvis loves to read. He loves to read anything, really, but he's particularly drawn to the *I Survived* series. He devours the historical accounts of some of our worst tragedies: 9/11, Titanic, Pompeii. He reads about war and stops in front of memorials to analyze the plaques, to scan the many, many names. It's as if survival is written in his DNA.

I ask Google, *What does IL-2 do?* It tries to retrain the immune system to attack the bad cells and leave the good. The body has created enemies, who knows how many, and now the body needs to destroy them.

What are the side effects, Google? Fever and chills, flushing, nausea, vomiting, low blood pressure, low blood count, change in mental status, memory loss, itching, mouth sores, poor appetite, fatigue, capillary leak syndrome. *What is capillary leak syndrome,* Google? It's fluid leaking from your veins into the tissue outside of the bloodstream. It's very low blood pressure. It's time to go to the ICU. It means Mom spends most of her treatment time with her system on the brink, near the edge. *We are trying to nearly kill you so that you can live.*

My husband, Brandon's grandma lived independently until she turned ninety. She used to spend the winters alone in Florida. She gardened daily, walked the mall, and practiced her geriatric exercises. "Don't laugh, Bran!" she'd say, mid-calf-raise. "This is why I'm still alive!"

To make it through as daughter watching Mom on Interleukin-2, I write the ways my God has been with me. It's Advent season, month of anticipation. We have much to hope for, much to wait for, much to long for. And so I write of pregnancies, miscarriages, temptations, Elvis's stay in the NICU, transition and crisis, mundane and mountain, every bruise, every valley, every major and minor moment, *God with me God with me God with me,* even when I couldn't see Him, or hear Him, or feel Him. *Do not be afraid. I am with you.* I pray it fiercely.

Sometimes Elvis makes so many enemies on the PS4, the thing starts to glitch. He jumps up and down, up and down, up and down, hitting buttons, firing, firing, firing. His guy dies and he regenerates. His guy dies and he regenerates. His guy dies and doesn't regenerate.

The Interleukin-2 didn't work.

There is research that shows children who experience trauma early in their lives—even before birth—have physiological changes to their brains that lead to an inability to cope with stressors, even the smallest kinks in their routines. Some of the symptoms are anxiety, fear, withdrawal, sadness, lack of self-confidence, poor appetite, low weight, digestive problems, stomachaches, headaches, nightmares, verbally abusing others. Excessive temper and demands for attention, aggression.

Ordinary Time

His guy dies.

From her cloud of Alzheimer's at the end of her bed where she sat, Great-Grandma smiled at me and repeated every five minutes, "I should be in the ground, pushing up daisies."

After his fits on the floor when I've said "no more," after I've let him be for a time, given him space to let his stress hormones simmer back to level, Elvis comes to me and leans in against my side, rests his head underneath my arm. I kiss the top of his head. I hold his face in the palms of my hands. *I love you, child.* It is over now.

So, what now?

"Pretend like I don't exist," Mom's doctor says, after the treatment is over, after it didn't work. Wait and see. Go away and live. Try to go back to normal. But normal is creased with pain and anguish. Normal is lined with panic. Normal knows nothing is known, nothing is predictable, nothing can be held as certain. There is no way to go back. There is only here. There is only going on.

I read *The Hunger Games* for some kind of escape and think about what draws us to dystopian novels. No one wants to hear about children being killed. No one wants to witness death—unimaginable, unutterable death. Unimaginable, unutterable trauma. And yet, as a preteen I sought out Holocaust stories. I devoured *1984* and *Brave New World* in high school. I wanted books in which most of the protagonists faced unbeatable odds, stories of tension and threat and persecution and perseverance. And victory.

"The thief comes only to steal and kill and destroy; I came that they may have life, and have it abundantly."[2]

※

He regenerates.

※

Tomorrow is my mom's birthday. She will be fifty-four. We will go to the theater and watch the sequel to a movie released fourteen years ago, the year Great-Grandma died. The great grandma in the sequel is still alive, still active, still the same actress witnessing all of these things with silence, with humor, with beauty, with grace. Not like some of the old people we know.

"Let's not be that way when we're old!" my mom says, and my heart clenches in my chest, my throat tightens.

Please. Please. Please. Please grow old. I take a sip of water. I force it back down, my terror, though maybe she sees it flash across my face.

Maybe she sees it and leaves it be.

2. John 10:10.

Soup: A History

REMEMBER cans of Campbell's tomato soup made with milk instead of water, and how good it was to dunk into that globulous, red-dye enhanced lake a triangle of Kraft American cheese melted between two slices of toasted Wonder bread, slathered in butter? That's nostalgia, right there—grilled nostalgia, nostalgia in a bowl you pick up with both hands to lap up the last drop your spoon can't handle.

    I tried to eat it again just a couple of weeks ago. It was grilled cheese and tomato soup day at the local university where I worked for a few weeks this fall. It seemed like a good idea at the time—the soup *and* the job—trying to go back to the way it was a decade ago. But guess what, you can't go back, not to previous jobs or previous lives, not even to grilled cheese and tomato soup, though I tried, and regretted it the rest of the afternoon. The university had given all its full-timers free meal swipes so that we'd mingle and maybe not feel so bad about dropping enrollment numbers and decreasing budgets—things I had forgotten I'd felt bad about all of the time the first time I worked for the university. I would be lying if I didn't say that the swipes helped. Fifteen free meals a semester with students and colleagues, and on top of that, at the same university I went to as an undergraduate! The same photos are still hanging on the walls of the student center from when I was a student. The place is dripping with nostalgia for me.

    I just can't tolerate dairy anymore, specifically cow's milk and sour cream and cream cheese and ice cream—basically any kind of softness. Parmesan cheese and cheddar, though, these are fine; they're tough and reasonable, not delicate things. If it isn't really real cheese, forget about it; forget about Kraft American cheese or Cheese Whiz or the equally globulous block of Velveeta cheese melted and mixed up with some chunks of broccoli or salsa (and half-and-half, and butter . . .). It's a wonder I'm not dead already from all the pseudo-dairy I consumed when I was younger.

It's sad, you know, because I used to love to eat clam chowders, potato soup, broccoli and cheese soup, mushroom soup, and of course tomato soup (made with milk). Now all these soups end in a filmy gurgle. It is the gunk and residue of regret, the aftertaste of nostalgia.

※

It's soup season now because the leaves are falling with the temperatures, daylight burns its wick down quicker than it did all summer, and most of all, I want to feel warm from the inside out.

Soup has a way of loosening things. Take, for instance, the sound every person on the planet makes upon taking their first sip of a really good soup. "Ahhhh," we exhale, letting go of the tight grip we have on our lives and surrendering to the pleasure of steam and heat. Perhaps you aren't an "Ahhh"-er; perhaps you are more of a "Mmmm"-er. Same effect. What you're doing right there is called in yoga the Ujjayi breath. The Ujjayi breath exhale is a purr, a whisper of air across the back of your throat that lifts up from your diaphragm and leaves your body, taking with it whatever tension you've been carrying unwittingly.

I haven't been practicing yoga as of late, but I still regularly practice my Ujjayi breath. The sound it makes in the deep center of my face takes me to ocean waves shifting and smoothing grains of sand on the beach. This time of year, the Ujjayi exhale sounds like a thousand copper oak leaves rustling in the autumn wind in their own last exhale of a long season. I listen to these leaves now that I am home again and not working at the job I tried to go back to four months ago. I've resumed the deck sky-watching and tree-listening and squirrel/bird/deer/groundhog-observing I had given up for a short stretch of time. I was not a good Ujjayi breather in my university office. Instead, I was a person who had to remind herself to inhale. I could have used a Post-it note tacked to my monitor as a reminder—BREATHE.

Now, though, I am back to breathing again, even if the bank account is tight. The frugality is worth the effort, because from the discipline of frugality comes the fruit of simplicity, and in this simplicity I've found my breath.

The name for God in Hebrew is not spoken but breathed—YHWH. Inhale *yah*, exhale *weh*, and now you have the name of God in your lungs, the breath of life breathed in and out, the breath of every living thing composed of the same basic elements that connect us. God in our first intake of air out of our mother's womb; God in our last sigh before the grave.

The pleasure and joy of soup is primal. When we take in the elements of a real bowl of soup, we're reuniting our body with its long earthy history. Broth has been around for thousands of years, originating from a time when people aimed to use every component of the creature they'd killed for nourishment, all the way down to their bones and ligaments. Our ancestors literally sucked the marrow out of life, roasting bones over campfires until the marrow flowed free. Soon, the pot came along, and people dropped their animal carcasses into a vat of water over a fire to boil all of that marrow-y goodness into a form you could drink.

"Ahhh," I exhale. Soup.

As part of our frugal meal plan in soup season, I make a pot of bone broth weekly. It's preceded by a whole roasted chicken, which we get from our good friend who is both pastor and organic poultry farmer. I prefer to roast chicken Greek-style, though we are not Greek, not even a little bit. The whole chicken gets a whole lemon shoved inside its emptied inner region. It's surrounded by two bulbs (yes, bulbs) of garlic sliced in half, then generously smothered with Himalayan sea salt, black pepper, and dried parsley.

Once we've eaten some of the chicken for dinner, I drop the leftover meat and bones into a pot and add the butt ends of celery, a quartered onion (skins and all), a couple bay leaves and some more dried parsley, and just one clove of garlic this time and let it simmer on the stove, sometimes for hours. When it's done and I've strained out the broth from the bones and vegetables, what's left is a pot of internationally acquired vitamins and minerals—hyperlocal chicken, Chinese garlic (I know homegrown would be even better, but a girl has to do what a girl has to do), salt mined in Pakistan's northern Punjab region, Florida lemons, and bay leaves, pepper, and parsley from wherever bay leaves, pepper, and parsley are grown. This international base fills my house with the aroma of home—a home much older and broader and more complex than the one we've made between these four walls, but also intimate and personal, the aroma of the home from which I came, the home I aim to create among my small cohort of humans.

Maybe the essence of all soup is nostalgia, a reaching backward in time and space to be reunited with the things that made us. You can translate soup into every language under the sun, and nearly every word for "soup" sounds like slurping up the last delicious drop.

As it simmers, I breathe in, *yah*, and breathe out, *weh*.

"Mmmmm."

✻

I hadn't planned to quit my job so suddenly after starting it. The plan had been to give it at least three months, enough time to get into a rhythm, enough time to judge whether I could do the job that provided stability and benefits in a tumultuous season while still doing what I loved to do, what I had been doing for eighteen months, which was, of course, writing.

For eighteen months, while I gave my body space to recover from long COVID, I wrote. I wrote web pages and social media content and email messages and blogs for steel manufacturers and senior living communities and mental health experts and packaging companies. I wrote movie reviews and book reviews and devotionals and feature articles about people who were saving the environment one solar panel, rain barrel, and community garden at a time. I wrote video scripts to recruit nursing students and undergraduate theater majors. And in between all of that I wrote and researched a novel about my grandparents.

But before all that, before I worked as a director of content marketing, before I worked as a managing editor, I worked as an administrator at a local university, a job I started nearly fifteen years ago and left seven years later. When my husband decided to go back to school, I checked to see if the local university was hiring, and lo, there was a job, and behold, I took it.

The week before I quit, I began to plan for a long-term grant that would support our department's literary ventures for the next five years. I began to plan for projects to expand the creative writing program from one degree-seeking endeavor to certificates in lots of other writing endeavors. I began to plan all of the ways I would stay, even though I was so tired at night, even though the part of my brain that used to be awesome at administration now just felt rickety and rusted out from whatever neural damage COVID caused. If you stepped on the floorboard of my brain in the wrong place, the whole thing might've bottomed out. I began to plan all of the ways I could stay, even though I couldn't do all of the writing I hoped I could still do. But it was okay. This was what grown-ups did, they *worked*, they *toiled*, this was their lot under the sun. And I had just turned forty, so it was time, for God's sake, to get back to what grown-ups do.

I said all this while holding my breath a lot, reminding myself to inhale. When I sat at my desk and worked, I breathed low, shallow, from a mostly deflated space. There was no *yah*, there was no *weh*. I decided to take a six-week class on meditation at our church, taught by my dear friend, George. George is a former Nazarene pastor, a hobby farmer, a spiritual director, a monastery visitor, and a follower of Richard Rohr. If there was anyone out there capable of it, George, I thought, could teach me a thing or two about remembering to breathe.

A couple of weeks into our class, and six weeks into my foray back in the world of academics, we sat in silence, meditating on Scripture. It was a psalm, but it wouldn't have mattered if the words were from a Disney movie or history textbook. All that mattered was the stillness, the breathing, *yah* ... *weh* ... In that silence, in those breaths, I heard, "Sarah, I gave you all of these opportunities to do the thing I made you to do with love and with joy and with freedom, and you chose stability and insurance." Inhale *goodness*, exhale *truth*.

So I sobbed a bunch, told my classmates I needed to quit my job, went for a walk with a friend during which I confessed all of my fears of disappointing people and my embarrassment about my short-term stint at the school, the glory and memories of the good ole days in my job, when I helped establish a writing community and made the program run, and then I tried my hardest to surrender over the opinions of every person at the university who mattered to me. When all of that was done, the tears stopped. The racing heart calmed.

And then I could breathe again.

Long before the "mmmm," long before the "ahhhh," the Ujjayi breath begins with a knife. I've peeled the carrots and onions, I've rinsed the grime that clings to the celery, I've prepped the requisite number of garlic cloves . . . now it's time for the dicing.

The music of vegetable chopping while the fat sizzles in the pot has its own rhythm of breath to it. I often catch myself counting silently in my head as I slice through carrots and celery sticks, 1 . . . 2 . . . 3 . . . 4 . . . like Lamaze breaths, short short short long. Preparing any meal is an opportunity to birth something new, to breathe it into existence so that it can be sustenance for some other breathing creature. Each meal is like a reenactment of the creation account. I have Douglas McKelvey's poem,

"A Liturgy for the Preparation of a Meal" within my view while I chop vegetables, measure spices, and stir the contents of my pot. "Let us invest in this preparation / a lovingkindness toward those / who will partake," writes McKelvey. "Meet us in the making of this meal, O Lord, / and make of it something more / than a mere nourishment for the body."[1]

It's this spirit I try to possess as I prepare most meals in our kitchen, with hopes that my people, whoever it is I'm feeding, can taste the love. I'm especially drawn to cooking new recipes, with fresh ingredients and lots of different herbs and spices. I like the challenge of making something from scratch.

The phrase "from scratch" comes from the scratch drawn in the dirt as the starting line of a foot race. A runner who "starts from scratch" begins at the beginning of the course, with no handicap. The Cambridge Dictionary says the phrase means, "from the beginning, without using anything that already exists."

No one can truly make anything from scratch. The whole universe was spun into existence billions of years ago, all elements woven together in a grand, interconnected quilt spread out over millions of light years and galaxies and stars. Even if you don't believe in a divine being who created all things, who are we kidding, to think we can make anything from nothing?

But I do get to partake in small acts of from scratch-ness, mini-moments of creation that are part of the cycle of birth, death, and resurrection. Each meal I make "from the beginning" uses ingredients that were once living, the flesh and substance of which will be used to keep other bodies alive. Someday, these bodies will give themselves over to earth, which will give itself over to grass, which will give itself over to animals, which will give themselves over to someone else—a circuit of harmonious sacrifice.

What has already gone before me to make this particular dish? Some farmer planted the seeds. Some butcher prepared the meat. Some honey bees pollinated the plant. Many things lifted their blossoms and followed the sun, waited for rain, and grew out of the minerals from which we all came. I get to partake in what has already been given up, "from the beginning." Cooking from scratch is humbling.

After making broth, my favorite moment in the kitchen with soup comes when the diced vegetables are tossed to sauté in the pot. Aromatics, they're called. After I scoop these fruits of the earth into my palms and dump them into the sizzling butter at the bottom of my pot, the whole

---

1. McKelvey, "A Liturgy for the Preparation of a Meal," *Every Moment Holy, Volume 1*.

house fills with the incense of their aroma, which lingers, sometimes for days.

I can't cook onions without thinking of my mom. When I was a very young child, for a very brief season I loved sautéed onions, of all things, all by themselves, cooked in a puddle of butter on the stove. Perhaps another mother would have scolded her silly daughter and asked her to just grab an apple or something easier, but not mine. She sliced and sautéed the onions until they were caramelized, just so, with a dash of salt. I can see her watching me with pleasure and delight, because that's what she has always done, gazed upon her daughter with pleasure and delight, a feature I've sought to mimic in my own household, though I often fail.

When my children ask a favor or a question, I default to "no" before I've even had a chance to consider their request. I dig in the garden of my roots to find the source of this impatient impulse. I find it first on my father's side, generations of "no's" when asking for permission to deviate off of a parent's path, but it's also there on my mother's side in the form of "shh," be quiet, don't tell. Obedience and shame are the inheritance my own mom has sought to shirk, so that out of her own work, this daughter is able to take a couple steps forward into freedom and wholeness. A couple more steps forward, and maybe this mother can make a way for her own daughter.

This work is not taught, it's absorbed, inhaled, part of the air that gives and defines life. In the grand scheme of things, it takes hardly any time at all to bring out the rich and deep flavor of aromatics, mere seconds until the sizzling garlic and onion aroma lifts, wafts, and lingers, lingers, lingers, carrying its healing properties deep inside our cells and blood vessels, becoming us.

When you finally finish putting all of your ingredients into the pot, the flavors have to marry. This happens with soups and chilis, stews and curries, when many distinct flavors combine to form one unique taste. Not unlike a lifelong partnership, the longer you marry the ingredients in soup, the fuller and richer and more indistinguishable the flavors. The flavors think alike and look alike, blending and meshing until even the vegetables themselves carry just one holistic flavor.

Today I am making chicken soup. Chicken soup is, of course, the soup I've been imagining throughout this entire essay, outside of the Campbell's can there at the beginning. Whole volumes of cheesy literature have been drafted, collected, and published in the name of *Chicken Soup for the Soul*. It is the great *minestra*, the queen of comfort foods, the nostalgia of nostalgias, the sultan of soups. Who among us doesn't have a sick day memory of a steaming bowl of chicken soup delivered by the hands of someone who loves you?

Each of us has our own chicken soup from which we came. I use my mom's recipe most of the time, but no matter how I try, it never tastes *exactly* like what she served me in an oversized soup bowl when I was a child. I want to replicate it. I want to step back in time and bring forward the aromas, the flavors, the exact proportion of salt, just the right heat, the slice of white bread glazed with butter dipped in to soak up the broth… but I can never get there.

Maybe the difference is in the water—hers directly from a well and ours piped through city streets, filtered and treated. Or maybe it's the types of pots we use, the type of heat we cook over, the material of the spoon used to stir and ladle. There's a whole world of differences between us that could explain why I can't make the same chicken soup she cooked.

Maybe it's something else, something that can never be duplicated because it exists in a moment long passed, a memory within our reach but just beyond our fingertips. No matter how delicious the recipe turns out, no matter how much I love the flavor combinations of exotic recipes, no matter how grateful I am for *this* soup, right now, it just isn't the same. I sigh, a deep, nostalgic sigh, a sigh for soup of yesteryear. A soup for days gone by. It's almost a Ujjayi sigh, no *yah* just *weh*, almost the breath of life.

Soup so close we can almost taste it.

The Body Is Not a Coffin

1.

In Port Clinton the weekend after the D&C, I wear shorts and a T-shirt and tour the islands with my husband. I look normal. But we only *sleep* in the bed at the B&B.

The room we rent explodes with lavender—it is flung in predictable patterns on the wallpaper and border; it is encased in cheap frames; it is on the sheets and comforter I ball up under. Lavender everywhere. The Egyptians used it for mummification. I was a tomb for the recently dead. Mary poured a pint of pure nard (spikenard, lavender oil) on Jesus' feet to anoint him for his burial. I have unwillingly spilled out that which was most precious to me, the desire of my heart. During the Great Plague of 1665, grave robbers used lavender combined with other potent herbs to wash their hands, a formula called *The Four Thieves*, thereby avoiding the deadly disease. I am a grave, and I have been raided.

And for centuries, lavender has been considered an aphrodisiac. Here in our queen-sized vacation rental bed, I yearn for my husband to turn and curl his torso against my back, wrap his arms around me, romance me. But, no. This is not allowed. I curl against the mattress, water the pillow's embroidered blossoms, and watch the lavender floral border bloom garishly—so many flowers, so many stinking beautiful flowers.

My mind plays table tennis with the facts of the last twelve weeks. I snuck Saltines and graham crackers into the landscape architect's office where I worked and hid them in my desk, hovered over the blueprint machine holding my breath so I wouldn't throw up. Was it the blueprint machine? Its repulsive chemical odor was sweet and heady even when I wasn't pregnant. The potassium ferricyanide and ammonium ferric citrate mixed together inside to impress the original image of a plan onto a new sheet of paper. The architect's plans were clear, defined, printed and distributed to the laborers so that what was envisioned for a landscape could become a reality. But sometimes the machine didn't work. Maybe the chemicals were low; maybe the bulb was too dim. The print's lines should have been stark against the white but instead were all faded and blending to blue across the page, too shaded for use and disposed in the trashcan in the corner. Something went wrong between the design and the copy. Something needed to be fixed before the plan could be properly reprinted.

It's another kind of chemical reaction that made the two blue lines appear in the window of my pregnancy tests. The stronger the concentration of hCG, the darker the positive blue line. I checked two tests to make doubly sure. By my twelve-week appointment, hormones rocked and heaved my system. I clutched a McDonald's bag of French fries and a McChicken sandwich and drank a medium orange drink in the waiting room, trying to stave off nausea.

Maybe my body was a lousy carrier, a poor environment with improper chemical compositions, unable to complete its assignments like a college kid in over her head, irresponsible, overwhelmed, failed, incomplete, did-not-complete, DNC. But "D&C" is not the diagnosis, it is the treatment. Dilation and curettage is the procedure used to treat miscarriages that occur after the first trimester. The cervix is dilated and the uterus is emptied of its contents. Miscarriage is spontaneous abortion, as if the body made a sudden decision to terminate. Through expectant management, the body is supposed to miscarry naturally, expel the tissue that was a developing baby all on its own. The womb is not supposed to be a coffin; it is not supposed to hang on to that which is lifeless.

※

A week after the procedure, in the shade of the landscape nursery yard at work I clip the dead leaves and wilted blossoms off roses, trim suckers and remove diseased stems from dozens of potted shrubs unready for a new landscape. I am methodical and ruthless with pruners. Some of the shrubs look unredeemable, but I trim anyway until there's just one short stump and a few small shoots protruding from the pot. Sometimes that is what it takes to make things heal.

Ordinary Time

The doctor's office number appears on my phone. I press it to my left ear with my shoulder and clip and prune, hold the stem in one hand and cut away with the other. The doctor is speaking about human substances and labs and procedures, blood work and chest X-rays. After the roses, I plan to split and repot dozens of black-eyed Susans the landscape crew brought back from a job. I think about transplants, the way cells can move from one living being to another, split, divide, and grow and split, divide, and die.

The fetus was a "partial mole" pregnancy, he says. The cells from the placenta could have spread, and the lungs would be the first place the cells might show up. Blood tests will let the doctor know if the pregnancy hormone levels are declining, a sign that the growth's tissue is gone. These tests will need to take place until there's no longer any sign of "hCG." There is an unlikely but possible chance that the cells from the placenta could "become malignant and spread." Potentially cancerous. I stand up with the pruners in my hand at my side.

"Can you start over?" I ask. "I don't think I understand what you just said. Anything you just said. Can you start over from the very beginning?"

I have never heard of a partial mole pregnancy or a complete molar pregnancy or an ectopic pregnancy or any other pregnancy-gone-wrong, and until I miscarried last week no one had ever told me things could fall apart like this. Suddenly women I know—my boss, my aunt, a friend from church—confide that they, too, had miscarried. These lost babies were secrets women kept and only shared once you joined the club. Why would you tell someone you miscarried for any other reason except to try to relieve the burden of grief with a little empathy, a little shared pain?

But no one has ever heard of a partial mole pregnancy.

I learn that a partial mole pregnancy is different from a complete molar pregnancy. Any molar pregnancy is a rare occurrence, especially in young women. On average, one out of four women miscarries. One out of 1,500 women experiences a molar pregnancy. One out of 10,000 women has a partial mole pregnancy. Molar pregnancies mimic the symptoms of pregnancy. In a complete molar pregnancy, the fetus doesn't develop at all; there is no embryo. The whole placenta grows rapidly into a cluster of grape-like tissue, which can expand to fill the uterus. If left untreated, these abnormal cells will bury themselves into surrounding organs.

This is what had happened with the black-eyed Susans; they had reseeded and spread throughout the landscape, intruded into other flowerbeds in a condominium park, and so our landscape crew dug them up.

What started as something beautiful and contained became invasive. There they are now, dirt loose and piled in front of the greenhouse, some wilting, some blooming, some with broken roots. The roses might have been diseased and dying, but at least they had stayed contained in their pots.

The doctor repeats his message and then hangs up. I stand in the yard a minute with my pruners, finish clipping the dead blossoms from rose stems. *Was there ever a baby?* I wonder, ashamed and embarrassed, *Did I imagine it?* I had dreamt of baby names; I had placed my hand with purpose on my small abdomen.

In the Bible, I read about a God who numbered the hairs on our heads before birth, who knew us before the creation of the Earth. That *must* mean it makes sense for me to imagine this bean as a child, this bean that stopped budding at seven weeks. And David, the same psalmist who thought about life before birth, begged and lamented for his child to live, the child borne by Bathsheba. But the baby died. The baby died, and David stepped out of his mourning, told those around him, "I will go to him, but he will not return to me."[1] Yes, this helps, not gone for good, just gone away.

But now I wonder, am I host to a different kind of growth?

In the case of a partial mole pregnancy, the egg is fertilized by two sperm, but instead of forming twins, the placenta becomes the molar growth. The fetus that forms is likely to have severe defects and probably could not survive outside of the womb. It had been a baby. We had miscarried. In the truck, driving with my husband throughout the summer and fall and into the winter, I lapse into silence, stare out the window. How could this happen? I had been so full of Adelaide or Rosalyn, Seth or Nathan.

In pictures by the beach four months later, I am thin and my sister-in-law is full, and we are both smiling because we are both excited for her and can't wait to meet the new little person who will emerge in just a few weeks. I want the blood tests for hCG to end so that we can begin again. The nurses prick my skin each week and then each month and measure my hormone levels. I leak atonement. This is my recompense for sins committed, I think, for sex I'd had before marriage, for the baby I had wished away, for the birth control I'd taken. Colleagues say everything happens for a reason. Yes, I think with my wrist facing the sky, yes, I think while the nurse works to

---

1. 2 Sam 12:23b.

find a vein, yes, God is justice and vengeance, fear and trembling. He is righteous and vindictive. Okay, here is my blood.

2.

Our dog, Tex, stares at me from the door. Crouched in this position, folded up in what yogis call the "child's pose," my calves and feet tingle. I collapsed here in a pile of boney and fleshy grief after leaving the bathroom again, "expectant management" doing its job all too adequately. It is the second time that I know I've been pregnant, and I'm miscarrying again. The carpet smells like dog dander and dust. How awkwardly Mary must have crouched at the feet of Jesus, the packed clay of the floor absorbing the lavender oil that flooded over his callouses, her hair pungent and overwhelming with this anointing oil, this sacrifice, this embalming. It cost so much. It seemed such a waste. The fragrance must have lingered forever.

This pregnancy ends earlier, maybe four weeks along, the size of a poppy seed in my uterus. A ballooned bundle of cells divided into two layers that don't even sound like a baby, *epiblast* and *hypoblast*, a POP! and then gone. I shouldn't have even known except, two days late, I took a pregnancy test. Two blue lines, a little light but defined. Then the spotting. Then the ultrasound. The technician said, "No baby," and I bled and bled. I'm still bleeding.

In this age of science and technology, why bow down when so much can be explained away? I have searched the internet for reasons why this happens—why we lose babies—but science gives no condolences, just hard facts about chromosomal and uterine abnormalities, cervix incompetency, immunologic disorders, untreated illnesses, polycystic ovary syndrome, bacterial infections. Science could tell me what might have happened but not why, why, *why* are they allowed to happen, why all of this brokenness and instrumental failure (abnormal, incompetent, disorder, illness, syndrome, infection, disease). How can *epiblast* and *hypoblast* mean *baby*, and why does this affect me so deeply?

The floor is soft and solid and I am weak against it. I know the statistics. One-in-four. One-in-four. Sometimes bowing comes naturally, a position you fold into like a child who just stumbled and fell, then was scooped up in the large embrace of a parent. Bowing is not always an act of obedience; it is sometimes an act of inevitability. *Why?* I cry, *Wasn't the first enough?*

On Valentine's Day eight weeks earlier, the doctor had popped a cyst the size of a golf ball on my left ovary through laparoscopic surgery. We had been expecting a grapefruit-sized cyst; we were prepared for the possibility that he might need to remove the ovary, or maybe even perform a hysterectomy, or that it could be something precancerous. So many unknowns to fear. Our pastor had prayed Isaiah over us in the waiting room, "Do not fear, for I have redeemed you; I have called you by name; you are Mine! When you pass through the waters, I will be with you; and through the rivers, they will not overwhelm you. When you walk through fire, you will not be scorched, nor will the flame burn you."[2] Isaiah says nothing about "if" you pass through the waters, nothing about "if" you walk through fire; it is a "when." It is inevitable, this brokenness.

After the procedure, my husband and I held each other and rejoiced. I felt the months of despair lift, a new hope for the future lighting between us—no cancer, no infertility, no permanent damage. *Now that this is behind us, we'll be able to start our family.*

But now my body cramps and crumples, heaps itself on the office floor of our house. *Didn't I learn enough? What did I miss the first time, Lord?* I beg, as if every event in life comes with an essay test at the end to assess whether you achieved success or whether you failed that lesson, whether you need another go around before you can pass to the next level. How many miscarriages would I have to go through before I understood, before God handed back the test with a baby-shaped sticker in the corner?

My boss has had six miscarriages. My colleague's wife had seventeen. When do you start to lose count? When do you begin to give up? Our friends and coworkers shrug, unsure, and say that God is sovereign. I know this. "I'll pull through," I tell them, and "Yes, God is sovereign," I say. Sovereign, as in the supreme authority, permanent authority, unmitigated authority. Who is this God that gives and then snatches away? Could it really be true that God causes tragedy so that He can make good things happen? Could He not make good things happen without first taking away something wonderful? *Who are you, anyway?* I don't believe Him anymore. What love is this that withholds the good, takes away the promise of babies over and over again?

---

2. Isa 43:1-2.

Ordinary Time

My women's small group at church commits to cross-stitch verses of Scripture. We will hang the word of God on the doorposts of our homes, weave the word of God into our hearts. Each week, we stitch a new verse. First, *Beloved, let us love one another*,[3] then *you shall love the Lord your God*[4] and *I AM THAT I AM*[5] and *worthy is the Lamb*[6] and *we will serve the Lord*[7], then *the fruit of the Spirit is love*[8] ... and *Jesus Christ is the same yesterday, today and forever*[9], and finally *delight yourself in the Lord and He will give you the desires of your heart.*[10] I curse, violently pushing the needle and thread through the cloth, "Delight yourself in the Lord. What the hell does that mean?" *Haven't I delighted?* I roll the needle between my fingers, rethread and thread again, count stitches and recite silently, *delight yourself in the Lord ... desires of your heart ... delight ... desire ... Lord ... Lord ... Lord, don't you see my desires?* Is God cruel or good? What does it mean for these seeds of life that seem to lift and rise on the breeze, to settle, to root, to die? I tighten the thread, pull each word in and through, stitch and stitch until finally it is finished and then I frame it, hang it in the living room where I can see it. But I don't know if I believe it.

At work I make a list of what I believe to be true about God and tape it to my computer, like a picture of a loved one I haven't seen in a long time. I think about Jesus' tears, how he wept with Mary and Martha after Lazarus's death, how the Son of Man did nothing to stop the dying, delayed His arrival and then cried with the sisters, grieved alongside them as they lamented, "Lord, if You had been here, my brother would not have died."[11] *Where were You in my moment of need?*

Even Jesus let Mary spill the lavender across His feet to prepare Him for burial. Even Jesus knelt in the garden, begged for this cup to be taken from Him, probably pressed his body prostrate on the knobby earth—and still nothing, still He stood, swept the pebbles off His knees and turned

---

3. 1 John 4:7.
4. Deut 6:5.
5. Exod 3:14 (KJV).
6. Rev 5:12.
7. Josh 24:15.
8. Gal 5:22.
9. Heb 13:8.
10. Ps 37:4.
11. John 11:21.

toward the night, cried from a cross, "My God, my God, why have you forsaken me?"[12]

I keep stitching.

3.

The Greeks and Romans used lavender to heal wounds. When we are finally cleared to try again, the months pass, marked by my periods. Easter Sunday comes and goes, but I feel like I am still on Easter Saturday, stuck between death and resurrection. Then gloomy April rain persists, the fog still thick, *Where are You?* constant. The question changes to *What are You doing?* in May. I hear, *I am about to do a new thing; now it springs forth, do you not perceive it? I will make a way in the wilderness and rivers in the desert.*[13] And I can feel it, perceive it, see the shadow of it coming like a wall of rain as a summer storm front approaches, only this storm is receding, finally. Branches break, electricity goes out, floods ensue, but the damage done in a storm is mercifully temporary; the new growth from the rain is lasting.

June perennials bloom; I plant Knock Out Roses and rhododendrons, transplant hostas, dig spaces for annual color in groups of threes and fives the way I had learned from the landscape architect. The landscape struggles at first, but with water and sun it thrives. By July, I joke about exorcising the fat and getting back into a spiritual discipline. I hear, *Therefore lift your drooping hands and strengthen your weak knees, and make straight paths for your feet, so that what is lame may not be put out of joint, but rather be healed.*[14] In August, I buy a size-six skirt at H&M on a trip to visit my friend Dana in New York City. I feel healthy and skinny and happy. Okay, I think, whatever happens to me will be okay.

And then I am a day late, and then another day late, and then another day late, and in my womb hope blossoms anew.

---

12. Mark 15:34.
13. Isa 43:19 (NRSV).
14. Heb 12:12–13 (NRSV).

4.

Somewhere a woman lifts her shirt and listens as the Doppler monitor picks up the slow chug of her own heartbeat and then something faster. It is the best sound in the world, or it is the worst sound in the world. Somewhere a woman holds a positive pregnancy test. It is the best news in the world, or it is the worst news in the world. In China, where families are fined for having more than one child, where one million are reportedly forced to abort annually, where boys are prized and expected to support their aging parents, a woman who tries for years to become pregnant is finally pregnant, with a girl. A girl.

Now what?

"You're *what?*"

"I'm pregnant," I tell my husband, the plastic wand I wish could abracadabra away the news I knew he'd hate to hear gripped in between my finger and thumb at my side. After our second miscarriage, it was six months before we conceived again. Our daughter was born in May 2006, and by November 2006 we were pregnant again with our son, who is now almost one.

My husband has been a full-time, stay-at-home dad for nine months, our agreement when I was offered an administrative position at a Midwestern university—I would pay the bills and he would raise our children. He grocery shops and launders and cooks. He potty trained our daughter, changes the dirty diapers of our son. After these months of constant fatherhood, he has applied for sales jobs, teaching jobs, driving jobs, coaching jobs, insurance jobs, and radio jobs. He has stood in pajama pants and a T-shirt mixing rice cereal and formula and watched me walk through the kitchen with my travel mug of tea, my makeup and styled hair, my high heels and dress pants and purse. He has slammed kitchen cabinets and cursed, "I hate my life!" before I could get out the door in the morning to walk to work to the job I love, the job that is the reason he is home with *them*, in this town without family or friends during this winter that has crept all the way into July.

"How could this happen? I thought you were on the Pill? Did you miss one?" he accuses, and I hear, *How did you let this happen?* I don't know what to do with this information; I don't know how it happened, I *am* on the Pill, I *haven't* missed a dose, at least I don't think. The air is dense in the kitchen and I open a window.

After work, we take our children to the park. Our two-year-old daughter circuits from the stairs to the tunnel to the bridge to the slide to the mulch to the stairs, while I push my almost one-year-old in the infant swing on the playground and he squeals and giggles.

I don't want this baby.
I want this baby.
I don't want this baby.
I want this baby.

I am going to have three children under three. My husband is going to leave me. I don't want this baby. What will we name it? I can't believe I'm even thinking I don't want this baby, that this timing is inconvenient, impossible, even.

My daughter is laughing and chatting incessantly.

My son gurgles and squeals as his tummy flips back and forth in the swing. It's been almost a year since he was pulled through the layers of my muscle and skin, almost a year since he gasped for breath but couldn't suck it in, nothing, nothing but screams, and they took him to the NICU for oxygen, surfactant, sedated him, tubes and machines and incubator, one among babies missing organs and pounds, babies born months too early, my heavy motionless full-term breathless silent baby flat on a receiving blanket in a plastic environment-controlled box. Here he is; he squeals and gurgles in the infant swing on the playground.

I want this baby. I want this baby.

"I want to warn you," the doctor says, "babies conceived on the Pill usually face complications early on and don't always make it. There's a higher chance of miscarriage." Ortho Tri-Cyclen contains two hormones, a progestin and an estrogen. Its business is prevention: when taken properly, it blocks the release of an egg during the menstrual cycle. Then, it thickens vaginal fluid in order to prevent sperm from reaching the egg if it should be released in spite of the first tackle. On the off chance that the ambitious ovum and a determined sperm meet under these conditions, the Pill also changes the lining of the uterus so that a fertilized egg cannot attach to the uterine wall. If a fertilized egg can't attach to the uterus, it passes out of the

Ordinary Time

body.[15] This little accidental embryo of mine has overcome every obstacle it's encountered. It means business, even if we quietly wish it didn't.

This is a new obstetrician in a smaller town. I hand him the encyclopedia of my medical history and he flicks through the manuscript, pauses every few pages, "and then you had a miscarriage? . . . And then how many to-term babies? . . . Oh, don't worry, the chances of another full-term baby being born with respiratory distress syndrome are slim . . ." and then hands the chart back to me. "This is probably better kept with you." The room feels too small. I miss my old doctor. The ultrasound measures six weeks instead of eight, and so we reschedule for two weeks later to try to find the tiny separate engine rumbling in my uterus.

At the park again to feed the ducks this time, we walk and hold our daughter's hand, push our son in the stroller. The ducks are territorial and herd their ducklings back to the water where they squawk and float away from the pond edge. Our daughter tosses bread crumbs into the water and the ducks gather near her. Solomon in Ecclesiastes insists in a cryptic verse, "Cast your bread on the surface of the waters, for you will find it after many days."[16] Sometimes I don't know what anything means, but I keep digging until I find something worth hanging onto. "This isn't going to be easy," my husband says. "But I'm coming to terms with it. It will be okay. We'll figure it out." We are all in.

At work I begin to cramp and spot. The ultrasound technician confirms that the embryo hasn't grown since the last review, and we schedule another D&C at the local hospital. But at home, I walk back and forth from the bathroom to the couch, weep as my body empties of its ashes. The couch is plush and I sink into its cushions. The body is not a coffin. My son and daughter crawl onto the couch and blanket me. I wanted this baby. I didn't want this baby. I wanted this baby. I didn't want this baby. This is a strange mercy, and I am humbled. I hold my children close, children I have been given when others were taken away, children of redemption. They are miracles of heaven and science, survive and thrive because of man, and God, and God through man.

I don't know anything about God's will, except this: love. Love each other the way He first loved us, with grace, and silence, and listening.

The Romans used lavender as an after-bath perfume they called *lavare*, Latin for "to wash," and I have been cleaned. Even though I'm sure it's

---

15. WebMD, "Ortho Tri-Cyclen Oral: Uses, Side Effects, Interactions."
16. Eccl 11:1.

passed already, blood run out and uterus empty, the doctor still wants to do the procedure. I emerge from the twilight to my husband's hand on mine. It is over.

5.

My son says, "Baby in heaven."

My daughter follows up with, "When the baby comes back from heaven and it grows up a little, it'll need baby spoons."

I think I must have planted these words, at least this sentiment, baby in heaven. They are almost four years old and almost three years old. My husband and I both smile and watch the two of them, hover in their conversation separate from emotional comprehension—*baby in heaven*—our eyes meeting and then wincing and then longing and then turning back to these two children and their finger food.

We talk about "the future" and "our plans" since this last miscarriage two weeks ago. I had heard the heartbeat, saw the seed on the ultrasound screen, returned to the doctor in Akron who frowned and said he was sorry, he knows how much we've been through. It is the sixth time I have known I was pregnant, the fourth time we have miscarried.

"I don't know if we will try again," I said. "This is getting hard. My husband is tired of this, tired of seeing me like this, tired of feeling like this."

But I'm not ready to say enough. These are our discussions and our separate inner monologues, as if we have any say in what comes from this womb, what will be birthed, what will die. As if my decisions mean anything at all.

But they do. I am ready to risk pouring out my heart, like lavender oil in a pot, before Him, ready to risk hope in the face of possible grief, possible disappointment. It means healing and embalming and cleansing and preparing and protecting; it is casting my bread upon the waters. Is it audacious to believe that this God cares deeply about me? Probably. But I believe anyway, in a loving, compassionate, patient, merciful, just, mysterious, powerful God of the universe and God of this dining room. He is the Spirit embodied in my daughter, preparing for the baby's return with spoons. He is ever-present and hears the prayers of our daughter for her long-gone dog, for the grandfather she never met, for the baby in heaven, and I hear these prayers and my spirit cracks and heals, cracks and heals.

Ordinary Time

He is the God who remembered Rachel, heard her and opened her womb.
I don't know what that means, but I feel the verbs: remember, hear, open.

Country Boys, City Boys

Country boys are tall—silo tall, not light pole tall—with a stride like they have nowhere to be. They are lean from lifting hay bales onto wagons in the summer heat; their sunburned skin is tight around muscle and bone. Dust and grease from the day's work is still embedded in the creases on their hands and the grooves in their jeans. They smell like life—sweat and sun and earth and oil.

After work and into the evening, country boys stand around in the shop drinking Miller Lite and smoking Winston cigarettes. The garage doors are open to the gravel driveway that crackles as other country boys pull up in their souped-up pickup trucks. They talk in that foreign language you've grown up hearing but somehow never learned, use words like "drivetrain" and "differential," "winch mounts," "trannies," "chassis," and "transfer case." They are trying to decide how to fix it. Sometimes "it" is the next day's job, sometimes it's the crops, sometimes it's a front loader, sometimes it's the weather—that foreman who dictates every task. Their dialogue rumbles low like warming engines, revs and roars as more beers from the rusted Frigidaire are poured.

You walk in through the garage doors, past the rows of rusted wrenches hanging off of rusty nails, past dusty workbenches and dusty toolboxes, welding masks and torches, air compressors and greasy vises, past the posters of half-naked women and NASCAR drivers to your father, the country boy born and raised an excavator on this very same plot of land.

It's been a long, hard day, as evidenced by the silence around the circle of men. You offer up a hug to your brother, whose muscles are firm and dependable, solid, tight around your shoulders. He smiles like all those country boys do, like they've got a secret they aren't telling you. You have

Ordinary Time

brought your kids to visit your father, their idol, who lifts them up into dump trucks and pulls the air horn. They squeal and bounce on the springy seats, sending clouds of dust into the air. He calls from the cab of the one-ton, "Breaker, breaker, 1–9. Got a copy? 10–4 good buddy, over and out," and the CB in the dump truck cackles and buzzes. Your children run from one machine to another, begging to sit in the driver's seat and touch the buttons that are able to move mountains, but the man who can make it happen holds the keys, and it's after-hours.

Instead, they climb into his red pickup, your son on the center armrest and your daughter in the passenger seat. They roll through the field, slow over bumps and rocks in the lanes, around the crops and back through the piles of stones and sand and land, past the graveyard of antique machinery. They unload and crawl reluctantly into the backseat of your sedan, which is neither dusty nor loud and doesn't smell like Pop-Pop. He waves and walks back into the shop. Your children whine as you head up to the house, leaving Grandpa and the country boys behind.

You are in middle school. It is "take your daughter to work" day, and your dad has rolled up in front of the school in the Mack dump truck. The chrome-plated bulldog hood ornament glistens in the early-morning sun. You might have glasses and braces, a gawky junior high girl with thick bangs and a greasy ponytail who smiles too easily, but your dad drives a dump truck. He shifts levers and presses pedals, and suddenly there's a pond, a basement, a driveway. He paves the way for your future. You stretch your leg as far up as you can and hoist yourself into the passenger seat, dropping your backpack full of books into the dirt of the cab. You hope a boy is watching, the boy whose name you inscribe in cursive letters inside your notebooks with "Mrs." in front. The truck rumbles to life and groans as your dad maneuvers the stick shift and clutch, and you buckle your belt, a whole day with Dad ahead.

Confined indoors, country boys fidget, flick through television channels, and then escape to garages, barns, and shops to tinker with something mechanical. Their homes are defined by metal, greased gears, and polished chrome; they shine in the late-day sun after being waxed. They roar and rumble over gravel, dirt, and asphalt; they require time, gas, and attention.

Home is the purr and hum of a Harley engine on the rolling Geauga County back roads, wind whipping against the face, arms and legs vibrating. Even though it's work, they are at home on excavators, bulldozers, and front loaders, too, content behind the wheel of a dump truck with a load of gravel or topsoil in the back. Their large, calloused hands wrap comfortably around the steering wheel of a tractor; they tilt back and around with ease to evaluate the angle of the plow and the straightness of their rows.

The house is not the country boy's home. When the country boy enters the kitchen, he leaves a trail of home behind him, tread-mark-shaped chunks of dried mud from his boots, dust shook loose from his flannel shirt and Farmall hat. He's tired. He slouches on a barstool and eats the food prepared for him. He slumps down onto the couch and turns on the TV to watch a race, a game, a fishing show, The Weather Channel, the news, volume loud because he's losing his hearing but won't admit it. In one smooth motion he hoists his legs up, arms crossed across his chest, hat pulled low over his eyes. Within minutes he's snoring, the broadcaster shouting to no one who's listening.

Country boys don't know how to relax but try anyway. They pack up their campers with four-wheelers and Harleys, drive through the night, ride all day, chop firewood, grill meat, drink beer, pack up and head out again. They spend long days driving for weeklong vacations at the beach and cut them two days short to get back for work. The trips are a competition to see how many sites they can visit in the shortest amount of time. They'll drive until they can't keep their eyes open anymore and then pull over at a rest area to sleep in the cab. If they think about staying at a hotel overnight it won't cross their minds until 10 p.m., and every place will flash "no vacancy" until 3 a.m., when they might as well drive on through.

These are the men you grow up with—men who fill dumpsters with empty aluminum cans of beer, who work, and work, and work, and then fall asleep on the couch. You break every smoke in packs of cigarettes, shake cans of beer you are sent to fetch to make them flat, anything to stop the country boy from self-destructing.

Country boys love the way they were taught to love—working it out, bringing it home, and turning it over to be converted into food and toys and clothes. But all you want is some time, the space to play a game of cards, a round of pool. Just a little more time—come earlier, stay longer, play another, best of five? Between the ages of fourteen and twenty, you date a steady stream of boys, are never without a boyfriend for longer than a week, stay together until it's toxic but don't leave until you find someone else to fill the gap.

※

You are dressed in a periwinkle blue high school band uniform and red feather plume. Your hair is tucked back in a French braid. Your black band shoes are a little tight, and the elastic straps of your spats are grass-stained after a long season. You have two red cords, one on each shoulder—you are a senior and you are a captain, a leader. The last two years, you were on the "other side," shaking your pom-poms, wearing sequined leotards and stage make-up in front of the marching band. You moved in choreographed fashion, smiled broadly in bright red lipstick, spent Friday nights underneath the lights terrified to miss a move or forget a step, to stand out from the crowd.

In defiance of cliques and social stereotypes, you quit the dance team the summer before your senior year and slip back into the anonymous ranks of the marching band. You take full ownership of the term, "band dork." From your position on the floor of the gym at the end of the football season, you scan the bleachers. There's your boyfriend, a trumpeter who graduated in the spring, who will take you out tonight in his purple pickup with the lift kit and monster-truck wheels. He has to hoist you up into the cab when you want to ride next to him on the bench seat. There are the other parents, moms and dads staggered in gendered patterns, mom dad, dad mom, mom dad. And there's your mom, alone, video camera in hand, panning the risers and focusing in and out as you play your part as second-chair first clarinet.

You knew he would probably not be sitting in the bleachers with the other parents wearing band parent T-shirts, and you were usually disappointed. But you could find him leaning on the fence by the home team end zone, watching from the sideline in the cool fall air. You knew he loved you. You found him in the shadows after the half-time shows, his strong arms tight around your shoulders, your band hat knocked crooked against his chest.

※

The country boy you date is like your dad—hard working and good with his hands, broad shouldered and tough. He showers you with gifts, buys you jewelry and clothes and bicycles and fancy meals and plane tickets. He converts his paycheck into love and you take it. He drinks. He smokes. He hides cans of chew from you. He touches you like you are precious after all and carries you up to his room. Your dad thinks he's the greatest. In the beginning so do you—he plants you on the coast of Lake Erie and holds you, listens to you, watches you, adores you. You watch the sunset with him. You read him your poetry and he draws you pictures of islands and sunsets. He takes you places you've never been. You are his center and he is yours.

But he only tolerates your faith and is on a crusade to find his Margaritaville, flying from Hawaii to Australia to New Zealand to Vietnam to Thailand and home and then off again. Meanwhile, you have never lived outside of Ohio. You attend school at a small Midwestern university, major in creative writing, read every book assigned in literature classes. You worship God on Sunday mornings and country boy the rest of the weekend. You try three times to transfer so you and he can be closer. You take a lot of things from him for a long time, give a lot of yourself with diminishing returns. It's okay, you think, you love him enough to make up for the rest. He works harder and harder to lose you, and you keep hanging on, expecting something to change. And then it does. And then you are through.

This is what you do when there are no country boys around: wake up at seven a.m., shower, eat breakfast alone, go back to your single dorm room, read your Bible, write in a prayer journal, listen to soft music about love that doesn't fail or let you down, read Faulkner and Dickinson and Milton, write papers, attend class, write for the college newspaper, go for an afternoon jog, take an afternoon nap, write poetry, edit the literary journal, write essays, eat lunch and dinner quickly, work in the writing center, study, study, study, lead a high school youth group, get a landscaping job, watch movies, spend time with your mom, close your dorm room door and go to sleep early. This is who you are when there are no country boys around.

City boy tucks his black button-down shirt into clean blue jeans. He's chiseled from backyard basketball, mornings walking eighteen holes of golf and evenings firing baseballs from home plate into the outfield. It's summer and he's a teacher off of work with nothing to do but play. He splashes cologne on his neck and pats his smooth skin with aftershave, grabs the keys to his black Ford Mustang, shifts the stick and drives to the Boot Scoot'n Saloon,

Ordinary Time

picking up his friend along the way. You've been waiting in the parking lot, propped on the hood of a '94 Ford Thunderbird. It's your first date with city boy at the line dancing bar, a place you went with a country boy once but all he did was drink while you tried to learn the steps.

City boy showed up at a church singles' cookout and escorted you out of an awkward corner. City boy laughed at the things you said, and you laughed at the things he said. He smiles broadly with his eyes, and you like him. City boy shows up again at Sunday school, runs to your car and invites you to lunch. City boy brings a book and makes you think he likes to read, which he does, but not the way *you* read. You are already reading into everything city boy says and does.

Tonight, you wore your tight blue jeans and white halter top. City boy is on the floor for every line dance, even "Long Legged Hannah (From Butte, Montana)," a jumpy, fast-moving dance performed by six or so seasoned line dancers and watched by the envying rest. Soon you've figured out the eight-count patterns and break down the steps to jump in for "Copperhead Road," and when "Steam" by Ty Herndon comes on, it only takes a couple rounds to master the grapevine, walk, and hip action that brings city boy up close behind. You silently thank your dance team captains for the lessons in hip gyration. When a waltz comes on, even though you don't know your way around the floor, city boy's grasp is firm on your waist and hand as he counts and leads, turns you back and forth, around and around, one-two-three, one-two-three, and just when you think you have it the song is over, the night is over, one-two-three, one-two-three, fingers braided and city boy escorts you out to your car, a hug and a peck on the lips goodnight.

You are impressed and proud of yourself that you didn't try to go further than that. And then you call, and call again, *can you come?* you call, and he comes. City boy plays softball with you, takes you to dinner, takes you to a movie, kisses you long against his car in the parking lot. He drinks, but not too much. He doesn't smoke. He doesn't hide things from you. He wants to spend time with you. He holds your hand while you worship together in church. He says he's sorry and that he'll try harder. He teaches you that saying "it's okay" is not the same as forgiveness, and you discover that you do not know how to forgive, that you have made excuses for bad behavior forever, said "it's okay," when it wasn't.

City boy has your heart, and you are chasing him down, hard. In ten months, you're engaged. In fourteen, you are married.

City boys are indoor boys—they are allergic to grass and hay and pollen—they do not lounge around the yard in the sun or sit outside at night, unless other people want to. They joke that their kind of camping is the Holiday Inn. City boys prefer climate control, windows closed, shades drawn to block the glare of the sun on the television. The TV is muted at commercial breaks, turned down low during Sunday afternoon naps, volume up loud for Monday night football. When a TV is unavailable, radio broadcasters are giving play-by-play and pre- and post-game analysis over headphones in the yard and speakers in the car.

Home is four walls and an entertainment set. It is a golf course in the morning when the dew is still on the grass, a tennis racket and a can of balls, ten guys playing a game of hoops in the afternoon, a beer and a hot dog at a baseball game. If they aren't playing it, they are refereeing it, watching it, recording it, coaching it. They sweat and then they shower—three times a day if they can. They make time to work out, make play a priority, talk about enrolling in a class at the local college to be eligible for intramurals. Competition is lifeblood and burns away the restlessness, and city boys play like it's work. They are never tired enough to turn down an invitation to compete.

City boys don't know how to fix things. When things are broken, country boys pull out their wrenches and start to meddle, even when they aren't the pros. In three months or three thousand miles, city boys take their cars to have the oil changed by a country boy. They call mechanics, plumbers, electricians, carpenters, and other handymen whenever something breaks. They pay the $8 to run the car through the carwash instead of getting out a soapy bucket and dishrag. It is easier to pay someone else to do it than to do it themselves.

City boys hang out, play video games, eat nachos, learn guitar, and smoke cigars. They drink pale ales and imports and microbrews, order mixed drinks at the bar and know which wine is best with prime rib. They will take you to eat Thai, Chinese, Italian, Japanese, steak or seafood. They love to explore new bars and restaurants in big cities. A weekend away with city boy involves dinner out, live music, and a nice hotel room with a king-size bed. City boys know how to relax. City boys know how to show you a good time.

Ordinary Time

It's the weekend before Christmas and you are pregnant with your third child, on your way to Nashville with the city boy. The getaway became a working holiday, but it's okay. You stay in Muscle Shoals at a fancy hotel on Friday, go shopping for a sexy maternity shirt, if one exists, and take a long bath in the room while you wait for him to come back. You do some reading and some writing, eat lunch at a Texas Roadhouse by yourself, and then he is done. He is stressed from work but coming down; you are excited and anticipating Saturday night. You drive from Muscle Shoals to Nashville and settle in your hotel, then go to dinner at Morton's Steakhouse and eat the most expensive and best steak and asparagus you've ever had. You go to the Wildhorse Saloon and hear great music, and even in your heels and off-balance body, you dance together, his cheek pressed against yours, his voice and breath warm against your ear. The next morning you tour the Country Music Hall of Fame, visit the Hank Williams Family Tradition exhibit and decide to name your unborn child Henry—Hank for short. Afterward, you hear a band whose bass player literally climbs the upright as he plucks away. Every song they play is better than the last. You both sing along, smile broadly, keep the beat with your feet. Each song is a track off of your marriage's soundtrack. You wish you could stay in the bar forever, walk the streets of Nashville alone together. But the weekend is over, and it's time to fly home to your family.

※

Today's schedule: Wake up at six a.m. Run. Shower. Eat. Feed the baby. Set out bowls of cereal for the kids. Make a mug of coffee for your husband and a cup of tea for you. Work eight to noon. Come home for lunch while city boy goes to play basketball. Work one to five. Take the kids for a walk while city boy cooks dinner. Eat dinner together. Bathe the children together. Sing and pray with the kids together. Put the kids to bed together. Feed the baby. Scroll through your Twitter feed, text message on your phone, and write a poem while city boy watches TV. Go to sleep. Lather, rinse, repeat.

You have been married for almost eight years, but it feels like more, or less, or not long enough, or too long. If your marriage is a topographical map, it would read mountain, valley, valley, mountain, valley, valley, mountain, mountain. You have three miraculous kids and have endured four miscarriages in between, and now you are done having babies, and you agree it's a good thing. There are seasons when you make love three or four times a week, take time to play golf together and eat out, laugh and share the same movie lines and jokes you've shared since you met. You speak to instead of at each other, you turn the TV off, set the phones on vibrate, crawl together into bed and roll toward the middle. You love him. He loves you. You are home.

City boy is good to you; he quit his teaching and coaching gig and stays at home with the kids so you could work a job that seemed to be built with you in mind. He buys the groceries, changes diapers, drops the kids off at preschool, borrows library books, loads the dishwasher, folds laundry, takes out the trash, and prepares edible meals. And more than that, he plays with your kids. He is the kind of father to your kids you wish your dad had been. You watch him bounce your baby boy on his arm, tickle your four-year-old son, and toss a baseball to your daughter, and you love him even more.

But you've been slipping from mountaintop into a valley. The last three months of your pregnancy and first two months of your maternity leave were celibate. You are five pounds away from your pre-pregnancy weight, back to working full-time, exercising when you can, and sneaking chocolate from the freezer. In the fall, city boy leaves on Thursday nights and comes home on Sunday afternoons to work his TV production gig for college football games, and you work Monday through Thursday. You can see what's coming because you've been here before.

It's Friday night and there are no lights on in the living room. The kids are all asleep. You are watching *Sleepless in Seattle* or *When Harry Met Sally* or *French Kiss* or *Julie and Julia*, sipping wine and eating chocolate. You are alone and lonely. During the week, conversations revolve around who needs to be where and when, what crazy thing happened with the kids today, and how much money is in your bank account. You feel unattractive. *You shouldn't feel that way,* he says, and he's right. You shouldn't. *You are fishing for compliments,* he says, and he's right. You are. In the darkness of the night when you confess your emptiness, he says he is sorry and that he'll try harder. It isn't okay, but you want to say it's okay. You are sorry, too, and you love him, you love your city boy, his patience, his attention, his heart. In the morning, you will make breakfast, feed the baby, hug your kids, and kiss the city boy goodbye, an "I love you" and "see you at lunch" on your lips on the way out the door.

Ordinary Time

City boy takes your daughter on a date night. When she comes downstairs in yet another dress, you scold her and ask why she changed, and she says, "I want to look beautiful for my date." She is your daughter, after all, and she wants to please her daddy. And she does—he tells her she is beautiful, assures her the dress is lovely without her prompting. He has a full night in mind that he planned—dinner at a restaurant of her choice and then a movie with popcorn and Sprite, her favorite, and maybe even ice cream later.

Country boy pulls your daughter and son up onto his lap and starts the tractor. They take turns driving around the yard in first gear, over the hill, around the apple tree and behind the barn. The sun's rays are caught in your daughter's hair and in your son's eyes. They are all grinning. Your son wants to be a "tractor man" someday, he says. He is a countrified city boy, pushes his bulldozers in a plastic sandbox. You can see him blending the landscape he's been given: He wears cowboy boots like his dad's and a John Deere shirt like his grandpa's, clips a tie to the pocket of his flannel shirt and talks in a serious voice, pretending to be Pop-Pop. When they are done driving around the yard, their hair smells like Pop-Pop—sweat and sun and earth and oil.

Your daughter and son both beg for love, shamelessly ask to be held, to be played with, to be complimented, to be adored, to be served, to be given gifts. *Love me, love me, love me!* and they do, those country and city boys, abundantly.

This is what country boys and city boys have in common: They hang out a lot with friends and drink and laugh and sometimes drink too much and stay out too late. They raise their voices about war and the president and football records, and don't you dare challenge them because they are right and you are wrong. They work hard when they work and play hard when they play. They are busy, too busy, way too busy, wish they weren't so busy, stay busy anyway, can't be anything but busy. And they are tired, so tired, really tired, exhausted from the sun, the work, the friends, the game, the party, the bar, the day, every single day, just plain tired.

As you pack up the kids, country boy folds his huge arms around them and then around you, and you breathe in all of that goodness, all of that life. The earth and sweat and sun and oil embeds itself in your clothes. His leather cheek bristles against yours, and he grunts out, "I love you. Be careful," he says. "Drive safe."

When city boy is gone, you run from preschool to daycare to work to lunch to work to soccer practice to dinner to baths to beds to silent living room and open laptop and glass of wine, to empty bed. There are days when you do not keep it together—you show up to practice ten minutes late, forget your daughter's soccer ball and water bottle, buy dinner at a fast-food restaurant, again, skip baths and send the kids straight to bed. And there are days when dinner is ready and eaten quickly, and you laugh and chase your older children around the yard, and you read them each a story they picked out, and you sing them to sleep, and you lay your infant son in his crib, and you softly shut the door and begin to weep, your heart so full it bursts in your chest.

When he is out of town, you miss him, but most of the time it's okay. You read books and write, return to the girl in the dorm room, remember who you are, apart from him and with him. You open the windows and let the sounds of the earth be your evening music, the crickets and the wind harmonizing with the creaks and rumbles of the house settling in for the night. The phone rings and you share about the hike in the woods with the kids, how your daughter chose the more challenging trails, how your son held your hand the whole way, how he tried the cucumbers and *liked* them, how Henry just fell asleep on your chest, his fat thighs tucked up close to his body, a pool of drool on your shoulder. You both laugh and say "I love you, I miss you, I'll see you tomorrow, good night."

City boys and country boys have this in common as well: they own and break your heart, but they can fix and fill it, too.

Little Joys: Music

I CHALLENGE you to find anything as magical as making music. You can gather a hundred high school musicians on a stage and, even though they resist cooperation in every other setting by their very nature of being teenagers, they will let down their need for individuality in order to lend their voice or instrument to a song. Politics, religion, ethnicity, gender, and physical appearance don't matter when you're cradling a French horn, embracing a clarinet, or sliding a bow across a violin's neck. What matters in that moment is listening to each other. Paying attention. And adding what you can to the song.

Somehow, these bundles of muscles, neurons, and lungs are able to process scales and notes, to memorize patterns, to coordinate their fingers and lips and breath to produce not just sound but pleasant sounds, harmonious sounds, sounds from over 1,500 different devices we've invented to create different tones and pitches at different volumes on different continents. And then, songwriters and composers had the brilliance to hold all of those different instruments and sounds in their head, hear how they might play off one another or with one another, and write notes so other people around the world could make their vision manifest into music, music others can perform, music others can sing.

What a joyful communion!

And this isn't just a one-time occurrence! We don't just have one song, like a third of songbirds, or even just five songs, like 20 percent of all bird species, or even 2,000 songs, like the brown thrasher—all of which we listen to and admire for their effortlessness and beauty.

Humans have hundreds of millions of songs. Even when we can't seem to remember where we placed our keys, we can store the melodies and lyrics of thousands of albums in our brains. We can mimic the crooners, sing along with the hit artists, make up our own melodies, and even use our voices as instruments in a capella choirs and for beatboxing. Song wriggles its way into our brains in the form of earworms. Song sidles down our arms and legs and makes our feet tap, our hands clap, the goosebumps rise on our skin. Song cracks open hardened hearts so we can feel again. Even the deaf *feel* music, play music, dance to music, and are moved by music.

Attending a concert is to join together in a choir celebrating our humanity and the sparks of divinity within us, singing with the same breath in one voice.

We're even able to record it and reproduce it, play it on repeat or shuffle, or go old school with a needle and turntable. We can find it wherever we go and carry it with us in our back pocket. We can listen alone or collectively, choose songs from a jukebox or be subject to the preferences of restaurant owners. We can tune in to hundreds of different radio stations carrying song waves on radio waves via distant satellites capturing the narratives of DJs and guest hosts situated in basement studios around the globe, and we can change the channel if we want to hear a different voice, a different song, a different genre, from a different place in time and space.

I play music all day, listen to instrumentals while I write, sing along to artists while I cook, and carry it with me while I fold laundry.

Music—like all art—is impractical. It doesn't matter in a material way. It isn't something we can hold, and even though we pay great amounts to access it, we really can't own it. And yet, can you imagine a more miserable existence than one without music? No music to create suspense or joy in a movie's soundtrack. No music to capture the particular spirit of a particular silent night during a particular holiday, which then becomes a universal expression of peace, of hope, of love. No music to soothe a crying infant. No music to celebrate a birthday. No music to carry the story of love lost, love sparked, friends gathered, long winters, cold drinks, or hot summers; no songs to get lost in, songs to find ourselves in.

What would life be without this wild, intentional, drumbeat-to-heartbeat movement collecting in our outer ears to collide with our eardrums that vibrate the waves to tiny bones in the middle ear so we can *hear* music?

How much richer and intimate life is with music, even this moment, washing dishes while my husband strums a guitar and writes lyrics in combinations that haven't yet existed, watching and participating in the act of creation, witnessing something becoming out of nothing.

Family Tradition

Grandma's piano is an elegy to Stephen Foster and Martin Luther. It cradles hymnals and folders of sheet music; it carries Christmas in its bench and decorates the house with its chords. We all sang around the living room, voices weak and strong, Grandma playing the piano, aunts embracing mandolins and guitars and accordions, Grandpa singing too, "Joy to the World" and "Hark, the Herald Angels Sing." As the colored lights twinkled on the tree, the gifts were exchanged, with Grandpa's perfectly scripted "Santa" on the labels, to each of his seven children and their spouses and their children.

How did we all fit in that space, the thermostat turned up and the side door open to let out the heat? Each of us cousins sat in our Christmas best, holiday dressed, lined up on the davenport with a pile of unopened presents in front of us, fidgeting for our turn to race to the tree and read the tag. "To Jimmy," I smiled, "from Santa." Then it was Jimmy's turn to pick a gift. It was never silent but we sang as night settled, we sang of silence—yes, there it is, in between "silent night" and "holy night," a pause, a peace, a quiet where we were each held in the leathery palm of Santa's hand.

Grandma (Jean) and Grandpa (Frank) met through a mutual friend who played music like they all did back then. Grandpa wasn't looking for a guitar player for his band—he needed a person to gather the accordion in her arms and squeeze—but Grandma played the guitar and knew a thing or two on the keys. Grandpa sang as Freight-Train Frank before World War II, with a band of farm boys who called themselves The New River Train Gang. While Grandma stayed back in her parents' blue farmhouse, Frank and Harry and Elwin and Bill wound their way around the country, playing bluegrass on stages and over the radio until they found themselves in Nashville outside the Opry with an invitation from Zeke Clements to play.

They were just a bunch of kids with instruments and dreams. Nashville! The Grand Ole Opry! All those rhinestones and ten-gallon hats! Their tour of the South must have been winding to an end, or maybe staying in Nashville meant more than just another night in Music City—something drove my grandfather to ask for permission. Maybe Great-Grandpa saw this as foolishness from one of his sons, gallivanting across the country playing music while there was work to do back on the farm in Ohio: corn to plant, cows to milk, fields to harvest. I trace my genealogy and family tax records and see with each generation: farmer, farmer, farmer, farmer.

Imagine the call home to Dad, the rush of adrenaline, the jitter of nerves, energy pulsating through phone lines strung from Opryland Drive back to Northeast Ohio. *Number please, LO 247*—were there others on the party line that night?

"Dad," he breathed. "Dad, Zeke Clements from the Grand Ole Opry has asked us to stay in Nashville, to play the Opry stage." All the static-filled silence between those miles, between the worn floorboards of the stage and the dusty ones in the barn. "Can we?"

"'We're going to fill the silo and we need your help,' his dad said, so home they went, and that was the end of that," Grandma tells me decades later, sitting under the canopy of a maple tree. The end of that. Harry and Bill and Elwin and Frank hitchhiked their way back to the fields of Ohio. To fill the silo.

It wasn't long after that Harry and Bill and Elwin and Frank all boarded planes for tours across the ocean, to the beaches of Europe and the Pacific. And that was the end of that.

※

Over roasted turkey, succotash, and Grandma's mashed potatoes, my aunts and dad unfold their memories of their father. "He packed a cooler full of Cokes every morning of each trip Out West, all seven of us kids in the back of a station wagon. When he got tired, he just pulled over, yanked an old army cot out of the back and took a nap right there on the side of the road. The seven of us sat sweating in the car, reaching our hands into that cooler of Cokes. There wasn't any A/C back then." They laugh and wipe tears away. I laugh, too, and take another serving of sweet potato casserole.

Ordinary Time

By the time I came around, the only version of Freight-Train Frank I knew was the one that slept in the barn, the one who doubled as Santa in a flannel shirt and belted brown pants, his green-billed John Deere cap loose on his crown. "How do you spell 'silk'?" Grandpa'd bark. "S-I-L-K," I'd reply. "What do cows drink?" he barked again, and I uttered, "Milk?" He laughed and I blinked, stumped by the joke he told me on repeat every time I saw him. (It was a trick, you see, a brain teaser because "silk" rhymes with "milk." Funny, right?)

Grandpa was a gruff old man with shuffling feet and scruffy white hair, watery eyes, paunchy the way a farmer comes to weight, around the middle, along the jaw line, but still packed tight and firm like a bale of hay. Instead of touring the country, he toured around the farm in his silver sedan like a bulldog prowls his property, around, around, around, traveling as fast as I pedaled on my bicycle, a hazard to drivers coming over the hill and down through the industrial strip of Munn Road. Grandpa didn't talk to me much, and even if he did I was too shy to reply, but every now and then, he gave me a random grin, woke from his resting position in the folding chair on the lawn and called, "Sare, run into the house and fetch me a glass of milk!"

Years had passed since some argument between Frank and Jean drove him out the farmhouse door, screen door catching on its spring, then clanking closed. Frank set up his ham radio and a mattress in the room in the barn to the right of the barn doors.

It must have been serious, right? or maybe just a misunderstanding, or maybe it was the kind of regret and anger and pride that simmers and burns inside a man, squelching mercy, forgiveness becoming a lost grace. Maybe he preferred the cold, silent room off the milking room to the hustle and bustle of the house. Or maybe he just refused to stop messing with that ham radio every night. Maybe he kept her awake. Maybe she's the one who said get out. I wandered as a child through the cluttered barn and milk house, dairy cows gone decades ago, concrete floor cracked in places, Freight-Train Frank and the farm animals all replaced by cobwebs and rats and weeds, and Grandpa.

How does a rift like this one form and never heal, the ground underneath the foundation of concrete freeze and then break? How is it, after all the years he lived in the barn, that I still don't know what drove him there, what kept him there?

There is a thirty-year gap between the man who drove his family of seven children and wife across the country and the grandpa I knew who slept in the folding chair in the yard. It is the same approximate distance as measured between Jean's frowning rolled eyes and Frank's sideways grin in photographs. The same distance marked by the limestone gravel sidewalk between the farmhouse and his bedroom in the barn, where the rats scurried across square beams and ate the grain that was stored there, silo filled and emptied, emptied and filled.

✻

"Don't write that down," Grandma says. We're sitting in lawn chairs around the old maple at the top of my parents' driveway, and I'm asking questions—how did you meet Grandpa, tell me about the farm, what's your earliest memory, when did you move into the house on the corner. Grandma's telling me about the turkey in the tree and the angry rooster in the coop, and out slips a low note.

I know the good stories. I have seen the way my family laughs together and celebrates the good times. There were many of them on the farm, many idyllic moments of pastoral joy. But I know there's more. Grandpa's dad—Great-Grandpa Frank, the same father who called Frank home to fill the silo—had a bad leg injury from a tractor accident. It doesn't seem like the kind of thing a family has to keep secret, but there's always more, when we want to keep things hidden. It wasn't the tractor accident but the silence afterward, the reasons why the doctor wasn't called, the beliefs and suspicions about modern medicine. Grandma's face gets serious. She frowns in disgust. "Don't write that down," she says.

What happened, Grandma? It is important to me to know. I know this, already: You rejected the Christian Scientists and went to the country Baptist church instead. Why does it have to be a secret? What happened, and how did it change you? How did it shape your children and by extension, your grandchildren . . . me? I want to ask, ache to ask—Why did Grandpa move into the barn? Why wouldn't he come back inside, even when he got sick decades later? What drove him from the house to sleep in all of that dust? Tell me, Grandma, what happened between you and him, what kind of a thing drives a man out of his house for so many years, what unforgivable infraction? Was it his decision or yours? And this, too: what kept him there? Why didn't he just . . . leave?

But I don't ask. Grandma's face relaxes. We're back to the turkey. "He waited in that tree on the hill for me every day, threatening with his wings spread wide . . . until Thanksgiving. Dad took care of him. We had a fine bird for dinner."

※

"Get me a glass of milk," Grandpa said, slouched in the lawn chair with his John Deere cap shading watery blue eyes and fuzzy white hair. I skittered into the house.

"Grandpa wants some milk," I told Grandma. Later, we'd continue collecting stamps, or maybe she'd tell me about my ancestry and we'd map out our roots on the family tree, or maybe she'd make me a slice of cinnamon toast, or maybe we'd practice on the piano. She reached for a cup, opened the refrigerator, and poured 2 percent from the plastic gallon. I carried it to him in the yard, and he drank it, lips dripping white. He handed the glass back to me and then lowered the brim of his hat to sleep, the afternoon sun high, and I skittered in again, inside, where Grandma waited.

※

Decades after he moved into the barn, they still played in the evenings, sometimes Grandma on the guitar, sometimes Grandma on the piano. Grandpa sang unexpectedly, like the sudden connection between the needle and the turntable, "Froggy went a courtin', he did ride, uh huh, uh huh," all talk on pause until he finished, "uh huh, uh huh," and slouched back into his position. Every morning, a glass of milk, a piece of toast, coffee percolating on the old white stove. He trudged up the limestone walk, up the colonial blue steps, through the screen door. Maybe a poached egg before he set off on the tour of Stafford and Munn. When he started to get sick, the patterns never changed. Grandpa refused to see a physician, but a friend who practiced medicine would come by the house sometimes to check on him. Grandma stood in the kitchen with the dirty dishes, then walked to the burn pile with last week's news, then to the compost heap with table scraps.

On some Sunday mornings I rode with her to the country Baptist church, her weathered hymnal in hand. The pastor noted the worship order on a placard in the corner by hymn number. I slid side to side on the smooth surface of the front pew and watched my grandmother's profile as she played, a wooden cross hanging behind her, *Amazing grace, how sweet* the sound that saved a wretch like me . . . I once was lost but now I'm found, was blind but now I see.

※

Grandpa passed away before the great-grandchildren came, sick and sicker and then so sick he *had* to come in the house, then out again to a nursing home, then finally to Auburn Cemetery where his body rests, an empty space in the headstone next to the etching, "Born Feb 20, 1920 Died June 3, 1997" between him and an overgrown rhododendron shrub.

I knew the man but I did not *know* the man.

When we visit the house, Grandma's piano is an ivory tombstone, holder of a folded American flag, showcase of black and white photographs next to colored ones of recent grandchildren and great-grandchildren. The age of the photographs varies but the faces look the same—see his nose, see her smile, see those curls? So many traits passed down, a certain kind of smile, long, thin fingers, good for playing the piano, good for stretching across the distances.

※

I used to peck out stories with my pointer finger. The keys barked like the tipper-tap of a snare drum, a *ratta-tat-tat* and then there were notes, words, sentences, and paragraphs. My teacher praised the stories and printed them on an inkjet printer in her classroom and then laminated the pages and bound them together. Young Author.

I wrote chapters and poems and papers. I learned the Power of the Pen in a program by the same name and placed first in storytelling in my seventh-grade district competition. I kept journals and recorded every breath and turn and thought and sight, even documented our family's trip Out West. I wanted to make Dad proud. National Honor Society, AP classes, clarinet, dance team, website, literary journal, GPA. Do more. Do more. Do more. Perform. Perform. Perform. *I'm so busy. I'm so overwhelmed. I'm so tired*, I said. *I made the honor society! I'm editing the website! I got a job! I got into Ashland!* "Dad, I got all As. Dad, I'm second-chair first clarinet. Dad, the web team won an award." Dad.

Today, I type like breathing, the *ratta-tat-tat* keeps pace as evidence of the grappling and reaching and singing I'm seeking, like breath of life from dust, like repenting, like prayer. I've watched the keyboard player at our church lead us into the deep places, his fingers and the keys secondary as the musical notes wear away our layers until we're in a thin place, the space where spirit meets Spirit, high and low notes resonating in a way that testifies to the true, the real, the pure, the beautiful. All of me singing *You give and take away, Lord blessed be your name* like melody, like harmony, and I know, I know I am made for this.

This is what I will tell my grown children gathered around the Thanksgiving dinner table years from now about their grandpa, when their children are shimmying against the seat and ready to eat dessert, this: Your Pop-Pop told the same "dam" joke for decades, about our trip Out West, going on the dam tour, looking for some dam bait, waiting in a dam line. He brought me down to his shop on Christmas Eve and we wrapped the presents he bought with each of us in mind; he passed me the Scotch tape when I asked for it, and I threw a roll of paper down to him; we played Santa Claus to the roar of the overhead furnace and the country Christmas music echoing out of the dusty boombox. One night, we drove all the way to Mentor to a department store to find the perfect present for Grandma Rose. Pop-Pop and Uncle Frank used to do the Cigarette Stomp dance, a slow twist of the leg and a grin to whatever music was playing. And there was always music playing. He lifted me up on barstools, lifted me up into the cab of his truck, lifted me up into the springy seat of the semi, lifted me up into his lap on the tractor. He lifted up my bushels full of sweet corn into the bed of the pickup each summer. He lifted me up.

They will nod and smile. They will ask for another serving of sweet potato casserole.

Standing in my parents' kitchen again as the kids rummage through my old books upstairs, Mom and I talk about the words I am writing, the stories I am revisiting. Do you remember the car Grandpa drove? Do *you* know why Grandpa slept in the barn? These aren't the stories we normally tell, I know this, but the silence grows enormous, swells and occupies the space between my cousins and me around the tree, Santa handing out Christmas presents to each and every relative, then shuffling back into the barn to sleep. How did we ever all fit in that space?

When Dad walks in, he rubs his belly and raises his chin. "Don't write anything about me."

He smiles.

※

My fingers tremble, the *ratta-tat-tat* slows to *largo*, decrescendos, then to *grave*. Insert here a caesura. Wait until the conductor signals. I am just a kid with an instrument and dreams, remembering, documenting . . . *Don't write anything about me.*

Nothing?

"You have to tell the whole story," my husband says. It is just us in our living room after the children have gone to bed. In our wedding photo on the wall we lean into each other, smile outward at the camera. There are no visible gaps between us. Brandon strums the twelve-string I got him for Christmas and practices an old Lee Roy Parnell song, "Saved by the Grace of Your Love." Some Sunday morning when he isn't out of town, he will sing and play in front of our church congregation, like my grandma did, but tonight, I close my eyes alone with him and listen to his voice.

I listen. But I break family tradition: I don't ask for permission.

The Empty Spaces

THE lion pride puzzle was a Christmas present that, at age eight, I must have insisted we begin assembling the second I opened it. Scattered on our dining room table for months, it was hard, and big, but I was up for the challenge. I sorted its hundreds of pieces into color-specific piles and negotiated our cereal bowls and spaghetti plates around its border, which you always finished first, of course, those flat edges framing in the future grassy savanna and blocking out our dinners. Each night and at every meal and every time I passed it, I would pause to push around the piled pieces until one surfaced, maybe, yes, that one, it goes right there!

Some nights after he smoothed and flattened the earth or dug a space for someone's new basement, my dad would hover, still in muddied jeans and a Carhartt. Some nights after she dried the dishes and cleaned the kitchen, my mom would wipe her hands on a towel and come over. Together we leaned toward the center, silent, sorting, sorting, then, *Here's one!* and we'd grin as the world came closer into focus, the sky above the lions filled with empty space, a pile of blue puzzle pieces, and possibility.

There will be two puzzles under our tree this year for my seven-year-old son and eight-year-old daughter, maybe a little harder, maybe a little bigger than they can handle alone. But that is why I am here. We'll lean toward the center of the table together and fill in the empty spaces.

Those Summers, These Days

ON a warm afternoon in August, almost all of the fifty or so members of my extended family gather at my grandma's farm to celebrate Grandma Fugman's eightieth birthday, and concurrently, my son Elvis's second birthday. Picnic tables and chairs dot the front lawn, burgers and hot dogs roast on a grill, a slight breeze rustles the century-old trees bordering the street. It is warm but not sweltering, cool enough to sit comfortably in the shade. Two of my cousins recline on a blanket with their six-month-old babies beneath the lane of maple trees along the south side of the yard. My dad and his brother sit at the picnic table, each with a Miller Lite in his hand. Some uncles and nephews kick a soccer ball around. While it's a special occasion that we're gathered for on this Sunday in August, one could expect to see a half dozen or so kids in the yard at Grandma's house on any given day. All of the family members on my dad's side live within thirty minutes of each other in Northeast Ohio, except for me, my husband, and my kids. Elvis and my daughter, Lydia, with my cousins and cousins' kids, push tractors and bulldozers in the same sandpile that my brothers and I played in twenty years ago, and my dad and his siblings twenty plus years before that. If they dig deep enough, they will probably unearth a Matchbox car from 1970. Beneath the shade of a maple tree, the cousins and second cousins and first cousins twice removed, or whatever they might be, get the same grit of the family farm beneath their fingernails.

I spent my childhood romping around the farm with my cousins, begged my dad to take me with him in the mornings to traverse the cool, wet terrain of the cornfield, dew heavy before the sun rose over the tree line. My cousins and I were taught the way to pull an ear of corn away from the stalk with a swift twist in order to make a clean break. After we filled the bushel baskets lining the dirt lane, Dad, or Frank or June or Connie or Rich or Pat or one of the other aunts and uncles, would lift the baskets over the edge of the pickup. We challenged each other to see who could launch themselves up into the truck bed the fastest. Our bony legs dangled over the tailgate, prune-y feet in wet shoes swinging back and forth as we bounced through the field to the house.

When we weren't trying to help pick corn or vegetables in the field, my older cousins and I would play a dozen different versions of tag, hide and seek, SPUD, ghost in the graveyard, and baseball, employing "ghost runners" when there weren't enough of us to run the bases, pitch, catch, and field. We jumped from the wooden bench swing into a mountain of maple leaves each fall. The swing's rope rubbed our palms until they stung as we spun each other around. We barrel rolled each other down the slope from the house to the trees, the whole world spinning. We picked red raspberries and black raspberries and didn't notice until much later the scratches on our legs from the bushes.

When we tired of playing in the yard, we walked through the corn and hay, down the hill, and into the woods. The trails wound randomly, looped around an ancient tree and backed up to a creek, but it was more fun to ignore the trail and plot out our own way, stepping on branches and startling at the sudden rustle of leaves nearby. The woods were never quiet, even when we would shush each other into silence and freeze, our breathing heavy as we eyed the forest for deer or fiercer wildlife we imagined into existence. The birds would chirrup, frogs ribbit, bees hum, chipmunks and squirrels rummage, leaves crackle. Cars could be heard coming down Stafford Road, spraying up limestone and tar as they sped along. When it was hot, we navigated skunk cabbage and may apples to the creek, waded in the cold, knee-high waters hunting for crawfish and minnows, challenged each other to walk through the culvert pipe underneath the road. As the pond my dad dug in the woods filled with rain water and runoff from the fields, I imagined all of us in speed boats, hanging out on a sandy beach, fishing and picnicking by the lake. It didn't matter that you could skip a rock from one end of the pond to another or that the mud bottom and snapping turtles prevented anyone except our black lab from swimming in it. We roamed around the pond hunting for tadpoles, wary of the higher weeds, afraid there might be snakes.

Our parents were elsewhere—working at a job, sitting in the living room with Grandma, weeding in the garden. We came back for lunch and for dinner, but no one scolded us for being gone so long, at least not that I remember. We were free to wander.

It is hard for me to imagine a childhood without the farm or a definition of home without the farm in it. The summer I turned ten, my parents bought the century home across the street from the farm and next door to my other set of grandparents. Home extended beyond the four walls of my parents' house and was defined by natural boundaries; it stretched through the field and woods all the way to the creek and then south to the lane, across the road and down to another creek, then back up through the rows of field corn to my mom's parents' yard, bordered by towering blue spruce trees. My brothers and I were more at home outdoors than in. No matter the day or season, someone was always around to play with; all I needed to do was cross the street, hop the ditch, and walk down the field. If there weren't cousins there yet, they'd be there soon, I was sure of it.

The sun is creeping into the west, and soon it will be time for us to load up our troop and head south. With the longest trip home, we're the first ones to leave. Elvis needs to be pried off of the John Deere tractor parked in the yard, and Lydia wants to play for just a little bit longer in the sandpile. They are fast friends with the cousins they see two to three times a year, and sometimes they remember names but often settle for "Hey you!" Their bedtime will come soon, and overtired kids are worse than kids who are upset that they have to leave grandma's house for their home in Ashland. I too am disappointed that we have to leave, and as I make the goodbye rounds, I survey the yard dotted with my large extended family and share the hope with my mom and dad that we can make the trip up again real soon, maybe Labor Day weekend. The limestone crunches underneath our tires as we back up and navigate through the other vehicles parked in the drive, pull away from the farm onto Stafford Road and then left down Munn and onward to the interstate.

Family gatherings almost always make me want to have more kids, even though we've made a decision to stop at three. Both Brandon and I come from larger extended families. My dad is one of seven children who range in age from sixty-three to forty-seven, five of whom have kids of their own. Strictly looking at age, there is no gap to separate the generations; our family flows seamlessly from my oldest aunt to my youngest son, Henry, born in grandma's 82nd year.

The number of children starts to trickle downward with my dad's generation; apparently, they began to ignore the command to "be fruitful and multiply," opting for the more manageable and fiscally conservative, "be fruitful and add." Many of my peers have thrown out the entire equation. The 1960 US census states that 22.6 percent of households reported five or more persons per household. In 2010, that figure dropped to 10 percent. As the number of siblings per household decreases, the portrait of the American family—and extended family—evolves. Couples are starting families later in life and choosing to have fewer kids, if any at all.

This shift is evident in our family. Counting spouses and not counting our cousins' kids, I have seventeen aunts and uncles and twenty-two cousins on my side of the family, and Brandon has ten aunts and uncles and sixteen cousins on his side. On the other hand, my three kids have two uncles and an aunt on my side, with hopes of cousins, someday, and an aunt and uncle and two cousins on my husband's side. And that's it. Our family is gradually shrinking.

As more families choose to have two or fewer children, the population is beginning to plateau. I don't know what that means economically, but I know for me it means a growing void. As our family ages and our grandparents pass away, there will come a time when the large extended family will no longer get together for every holiday; with the patriarchs and matriarchs alive only in our jokes and memories, we will eventually begin to celebrate special occasions with our more immediate family. Fifty of my grandma's descendants attended her 80th birthday party. Today, celebrating my dad's birthday with just his offspring would include five children and three grandchildren.

I find myself sighing just thinking about it. What will my children's memories of growing up look like without this huge extended family experience? Will we all keep getting together even as our families grow apart, or will our sheer numbers limit us from coming together in this way? And when I am the matriarch, will I be able to look out across the yard and smile with satisfaction at the screaming grandchildren and great-grandchildren hopping about like bunnies in the grass, my own kids doing their best to herd their flock toward dinner plates piled with potato salad and baked beans? Or will we all be cities and states away for holidays, off creating our own definitions of home and family in unfamiliar towns?

Those Summers, These Days

The small strip of land at the back of our city lot slopes downhill and collides with the open pasture owned by the city, known as Freer Field. Aside from the one time a year when we play beanbag toss or horseshoes, the narrow area is useless as far as yard space is concerned and is a pain to mow. To make better use out of it, we borrowed a friend's tiller and made ourselves a garden. I'm listening to Johnny Cash sing about the cotton fields back home as I weed between the rows of vegetables we started from seed this year. It is a meager garden, at six feet by twenty feet, half of which is pepper plants I'm afraid I started too late to bear any fruit. The rest is a row of cilantro, three rows of cucumbers, and nine—*nine*—zucchini plants. We'll be handing out bushels of zucchini to anyone who will take them.

It doesn't take too long to finish weeding the six short rows, but even so I've worked up a good sweat. My newborn will be awake and ready to eat soon, so I gather up my garden hoe, gloves, and phone and walk thirty feet to the garage and then the remaining ten to the back door. In the late afternoon, my two oldest kids haul the hose around the yard with me to water all our plants, from the purple petunias and sweet potato vines around front to the sunflowers and vegetable garden in back. In order to make sure they get a good soak instead of a frenetic sprinkle, the kids count to twenty for each plant. It certainly isn't anything like the cornfields back home, but we dug up the turf, pulled the weeds, tilled the soil, and sowed the seeds ourselves, and with any good fortune and some sunshine, we might even reap a harvest.

My memories of childhood on my grandma's farm are romantic and wrapped in nostalgia, and I know it. The truth is, farm life is hard. For every sun-filled morning in the rows of corn, there's a hot and sticky afternoon picking rocks and raking dust. The deer are eating the corn, the raccoons are eating the corn, the earworms are eating the corn, and someone needs to do something about it.

The garden at my grandma's takes all day to weed and three long hours to pick. In order to be ready to sell produce at the corner stand by noon and to avoid as much heat as possible, my Aunt Carolyn begins picking by 8 a.m. She wears a light, short-sleeved, button-down blouse and a flowing skirt, her strawberry blonde hair pulled back with a large clip. Loose strands fall around her face. She wears glasses that hide startling blue eyes and no makeup. Of course she is beautiful; she is a Fugman girl in the field on a hot summer day.

Most of the morning is spent bent over at the waist with a sharp paring knife cutting loose cucumber, zucchini, several varieties of squash and peppers, green beans, and tomatoes. As the season progresses it becomes harder and harder to navigate the jungle of vegetables. The tomatoes that have fallen off or are left unpicked begin to rot, and vines of various squash weave themselves across what used to be clear rows. After picking, the vegetables are loaded into the back of my aunt's car and if there's room, stacked on top of the truck bed of corn. Aunt June rinses away the mud and sweat from the field and changes into a soft white blouse and blue jeans, dries her blonde hair and applies makeup, even though she doesn't need it. After a quick cup of coffee, she's off in the Chevy to set up the produce stand.

A new generation of cousins hangs out at the produce stand these days, but it doesn't seem like that long ago since I sat in a folding chair under a red canopy and helped make change for customers who stopped for a dozen ears of corn and a quart container of tomatoes. The stand was situated at the corner of Route 44 and East Washington Street, across from Auburn Inn and catty-corner to a bait and tackle shop. East Washington dead ends into Lake LaDue, a 1500-acre reservoir with twenty miles of shoreline constructed in 1963 to provide additional water supply to Akron. Optimistic fishermen with coolers potentially full of largemouth bass, bluegill, yellow perch, walleye, and catfish often stopped at the stand on their way home from a day out on the lake.

Those summers at the produce stand, my cousins and I ate Doritos and drank Pepsi while we sat on the sticky vinyl bench seat in the cab of the pickup. We polished the dirt off of the vegetables and arranged the quart containers on the checkered tablecloth. We counted cars as they drove by. We raked the tire tracks out of the dirt. We moseyed into Auburn Inn and talked with the bartender while we waited for a burger. We tried to find a home for an abandoned kitten. We filled a lot of bushels and bagged a lot of corn. We sat on the tailgate munching fruit, letting the peach juice drip on our thighs.

These days, the youngest of my cousins might hang out, but mostly it's my Aunt June and her sisters, Connie and Carolyn, the oldest of my dad's sisters, who run the corner stand, and by extension, the front-end of the family farm. My dad's youngest sister and her family recently built a house in a clearing at the bottom of the hill, where the field meets the woods. They moved from Akron, in a house not too far away from where Brandon and I lived when we first got married. Her five kids are the youngest of my cousins, ranging in age from eighteen to six, and they have carried on the family tradition of romping around the farm. When I come home to visit my parents and I drive by my grandma's farmhouse, there's often a cousin or two playing in the yard. My aunt says this is why they moved home, so that her kids could have this same experience.

I've only been a visitor the last twenty years. The farm isn't a source of income for me, it is a park I can bring my kids on the weekends to pick a few ears of sweet corn and gallivant around the woods. I am nearing thirty and live seventy miles from the farm. My kids will grow up making field trips to Auburn, visiting local pick-your-own and petting zoo farms, returning to our brick bungalow in the evenings. We'll maintain our six-foot by twenty-foot garden that stretches across our postage-stamp property and grow vegetables recreationally.

※

When I was in middle school, the land adjacent to the farm's woods was sold to developers, and houses situated around a cul-de-sac on three-acre lots began to pop up. Shortly thereafter, the Timmons family sold the fields around my parents' house, too. Soon we had neighbors where we used to have field corn and hay. I can only imagine what the neighbors thought of us the day two of our four hogs got loose and trotted through their backyards. Industry and development are encroaching on our family's property. Semi-trucks tear up and down Munn Road hauling whatever it is that Johnson Plastics, Mar-Bal, and Johnsonite manufacture, and new industrial parkways cut into what used to be farmland and forest along the road to my parents' house.

I know I'm not the only one in the United States who experiences the family farm as a dying tourist attraction or an endangered species in the zoo of American lifestyles. Of the 43.4 million estimated United States households in 1950, 25 percent were farmers. In 2007, the percentage of farming households dropped to 1.9 percent. The family farm is becoming a museum of occupational artifacts—check out the dairy cow, the pigpen, plow blades, rusted fenders, abandoned tillers, the aging man with the overalls and John Deere hat, and up these stairs, the rotting floorboards of the hayloft—watch your step, you might fall through the mirage of pastoral romanticism.

Under 2 percent of the households in America experience firsthand the early morning dew on the crops, the warm smell of oats and barley mixed with straw and manure, the clip-clop of a horse's hooves down the center aisle of the paddocks, the hungry grunt of a hog rummaging your palm for cornmeal . . . and it is likely that percentage will continue to decline. A portion of the remaining 98 percent might like the idea of rural living and move into their new McMansions in the developments named after the landscape, but they didn't buy their houses on days when they were standing downwind from the dairy barn.

Our household falls in the non-farming 98 percent, though my son vows to become a "tractor man" like his grandpa someday. From this plot of land, the best training we can give is a sandbox, some die-cast tractors, and regular weekend trips up I-71.

※

We relocated to Ashland (pop. 21,741) four years ago after living in Akron, a city of over 200,000. There are 3,338 people per square mile in Akron, people squeezed into apartments, people smooshed between rubber-city bungalows, people leaning over fences and off sidewalks into the pothole ridden streets. People are always everywhere, walking underneath the city lights to the 24-hour pharmacy or grocery or bar or greasy-spoon diner, heard laughing and yelling through the closed doors and windows of your home in the middle of the night.

Ashland's 2,099 people per square mile doesn't have anything on Auburn Township's 185, but it's open country compared to our colonial in Akron that seemed barricaded by cheap renovations, run-down bungalows, and newly transplanted mobile homes. The air in Ashland is not as stifling, the summer heat does not ricochet off every paved square inch of city street, the road crews wait to spray salt and ash until it's absolutely necessary, because, let's face it, most of us in small towns aren't in a hurry to get anywhere in a snowstorm.

When the plow trucks forgot to make it down our street in Akron in the winter, it was because of where we were in the city. There are currently 118 registered sex offenders within a two-mile radius of our old address in Akron. I know this because we signed up for an automatic email that alerted us when a sex offender moved into our neighborhood. Our next-door neighbors struggled with drug and alcohol addictions, kicked each other out of the house, beat their dogs, yelled at their kids, and abandoned cars on the side of the street. They also ran daycares out of their homes, worked moving-truck jobs and nursing jobs and assembly line jobs, first-, second-, and third-shift jobs, multiple jobs and lousy hours to support their families. They planted silk flowers in their yards, painted their fences, and pruned the yews and boxwoods into geometric shapes. They lived in the same house for sixty years with their spouses and watched the neighborhood change. The people around us were, for the most part, hardworking, blue-collar families, battling against debt and luck and bad decisions and poor educational systems.

Everyone's business was up in everyone else's business, but we were all in that neighborhood together. If you nodded and smiled and knew Jake's kid's kids' names, you might as well be blood relatives. But there were those few houses with those few people, men in "wifebeaters" on rotting front porches, men who looked at you for a long time without saying anything as you walked by, men who did not blink or smile or frown, men who just stood there. Most of the time, though, I felt safe. We had two seventy-pound coonhounds and a fenced-in backyard. But when we found out that our family was going to grow beyond the two of us and our dogs, the neighborhood bruises started to matter a little more. I couldn't imagine walking my children up and down the sidewalks, cutting through crowds of teenage boys. What are they doing, standing around in front of their houses like that all of the time? Who is the man in the Cadillac that pulls up on random afternoons?

※

Ashland isn't exactly the city. It's the town of no fences, the "world headquarters of nice people" (says a billboard off of I-71). Avenues and streets are lined with mature little-leaf lindens and maples and oaks. While our yard in Ashland is about one-tenth of an acre and nearly every square foot is sculpted and manicured, we have our garden, and behind our plot of land is the city-owned field. Beyond the field is an expanse of woods, gravel trails woven in and through. Reclining in a lawn chair on the patio in the summer evenings with tiki torches lit, staring out across the yard, Ashland feels a little like Auburn. We let our kids run out to an electric pole, almost to the woods, and back. They often stop to pick a bouquet of dandelions or clover, depending on the season. Theirs is a smaller version of my childhood independence, the freedom to roam a plot of land that seemed wild and endless.

I'm on maternity leave this summer. It is our fourth year here after relocating for a job at the university. Once Henry wakes up, the kids get out their bicycles and the five of us head down the street. Lydia and Elvis laugh and scream down the sloping sidewalk, shouting out hellos to each of our neighbors, whom we know by first name. They wait for us to catch up to them at the intersection so we can cross Morgan Avenue to our friends' house on the corner of Morgan and Chestnut. The kids get a kick out of running up to our friends' front door, ringing the doorbell, and then running away to try climbing the magnolia tree in the side yard. Miles and LeeAnn open the door, and we chat about church, work, upcoming barbecue nights, books, and so on. Brandon and I round up the tree-climbers and continue on our walk toward the seminary park, a small playground adjacent to apartments on the seminary's campus. The kids continue squealing and laughing as they chase each other up and around the playground equipment. Brandon and I sit down at a picnic table in the shade. Some of our friends are students at the seminary, and we keep watch in the parking lot for their cars. We decide to see if Tony and Jillian want to grill out and send them a text message, shepherding Elvis and Lydia back to their bikes. On the way home, a car honks and an arm reaches out the driver's side to wave and we wave back, sure we know the man attached to the hand.

The grill is hot and barbecue chicken is sizzling. A casserole of zucchini we just picked and eggplant from another friend's garden is bubbling and ready to be pulled out of the oven. Tony and Jillian brought green beans from their garden, too. Elvis and Lydia race around the house in their Power Wheels modeled after the kind of equipment you might see in the yard at the farm—a John Deere Gator and silver Ford F-150—with a couple of baby dolls hanging out the back. Elvis is sporting a pirate hat and sword, Lydia has on her Belle dress, and both are wearing cowboy boots handed down from Brandon's cousin's kids. It's a cool, clear summer evening, a whisper of fall in the breeze. After dinner, we all decide to go to the Red Barn at Brookside Park for generous servings of ice cream, and there's an Army Corps brass band playing at the Myers Bandshell. Lydia practices being a ballerina in the grass, and as the band plays "Yankee Doodle Dandy," another set of friends walks up with their lawn chairs for date night. There's more chatting and smiling and waving at passersby we recognize from our jobs, our street, our schools, our church—and then it's time to head home to bed.

Tonight, I am grateful for the brick patio and cozy backyard with the vining petunias, Stella d'Oro Daylilies, and Knock Out Roses, grateful for the kids doing laps and the husband cracking jokes at the grill, grateful for fenceless backyards and community parks and large portions of ice cream, grateful for these friends within walking distance of our home whose blood relatives live out of town like ours. We have adopted each other as part of our Ashland family.

The open spaces of my childhood are becoming more rare and sweet. The farther from the fields I get, the more I look back, and yet it isn't the hills and dales that I want to run to, it's the little girl and her herd of cousins around the canopy on the corner selling vegetables with her aunts. She is surrounded by familial life, supported and loved in spite of her insecurities, embraced, for better or worse, by a single rural culture. She doesn't know that 98 percent of the population hasn't navigated through a field of corn in a beat-up S-10 pickup truck. She isn't aware that most kids only see their cousins on holidays and certainly don't spend their Saturday mornings picking vegetables together. There's no such thing as "family reunion" in her vocabulary—the family is always reunion-ing. They celebrate every holiday and birthday at a relative's, spontaneously flock to the living room of their grandma's house. There is something in her core that longs for the presence and stability of family. She'll realize this as a hardworking, well-educated adult, plugging away in a private office on a university campus, standing miles from all of her family in the front yard of her little house with three children of her own.

My three kids will experience their childhood differently than the way I experienced childhood. Perhaps they will remember the late afternoon walks down Morgan and over to Samaritan Avenue, or strolling to the university and riding bikes in circles around the flagpole on the quad. Or maybe they will remember walking across the field to the edge of the woods behind our house to pick the raspberries growing in massive, wild tangles. They'll probably have a collective memory of the hot-air balloon festival in the field on the Fourth of July weekend, and the fireworks show from our friends'

backyard. Maybe they will remember grilling out with all our friends every Thursday night, or walking to friends' houses on a whim. Certainly they will remember playing in the sandpile at Grandma's house, swinging from the rope swing tied to a branch in the maple tree, riding the tractor around the lawn. I want to give them all of this—the farm, the town, the friends, the family, love braided and woven between each memory.

On the way home from the farm, our kids accordion-ed against each other asleep in the back seat, I watch the suburban sprawl give way again to rural fields, tractors tilling up soil, horses grazing in pastures, barns casting long shadows across the earth. The highway divides the farmland into strips pockmarked with light poles and billboards. It stretches in a long diagonal line from Auburn to Ashland. It is this interstate that makes this day trip possible. Brandon and I hold hands between the seats and sing along to some country song about watching corn pop up in rows. We take turns looking behind us into the back seat at our tired children and steer our car home.

The Lord's Name

In memory of Brian Doyle

"Jesus" feels like sandpaper against the roof of my mouth these days because I'm so out of practice saying the name. I'd like a new name for a while. Maybe Bob, Lisa, or Mister Louie, the name given by Brian Doyle's Sunday School class he wrote about in a short essay once. Any other name, except the one thrown about on placards and Hallmark cards, careless and whitewashed, reeking of pastels and artificial rose-scented soap. Something unusual and refreshing, something as unexpected and revolutionary as the actual Man-God that touched untouchables, talked to unspeakables, taught unteachables, healed unhealables.

When great and beautiful things would happen, we would say "Praise Mister Louie!" It would be new and unusual enough to maybe matter, maybe even tweak a nerve connection between heart and mind, maybe make us think or feel or do a little something, feel a little something more than wariness at this idol we've made of a name. Which Jesus are you referring to just now?

These days I don't feel like I follow the same Jesus some people say they follow, so I avoid the name altogether, opt for "Christ-follower" as if that's any better, or call myself "spiritual" instead of religious, say I'm on a "journey of faith" instead of "I'm a Christian," preach Love as the Way, the Truth, and the Life instead of just swearing allegiance to this name. It's this amped-up commitment to try to follow more closely the Son of Man, One Who Sees, Lamb of God that has caused some followers of Jesus to question my salvation. They are concerned when I doubt the existence of an eternal lake of fire, an eternal separation from Love Incarnate, even though Paul in the New Testament says he's "convinced that neither death, nor life, nor angels, nor principalities, nor things present, nor things to come, nor powers, nor height, nor depth, nor any other created thing, will be able to separate us from the love of God, which is in Christ Jesus our Lord."[1]

They worry over my soul. I am "losing my religion." I am "drifting in a wake of godlessness." I have become "too afflicted with the world." Have I forgotten my Jesus, have I "given the devil a foothold," have I renounced my faith in the saving name, the name above all names?

Sometimes when a name is so stained, you need a revelation, a revolution of thought to upturn the tables set up to sell forgiveness.

"MISTER LOUIE LOVES YOU!"

Brian Doyle's Mister Louie isn't *that* much of a stretch. They didn't even call him "Jesus" when he walked around Judea. *Yeshua* translates from Hebrew to the English *Joshua*, from the Greek *Iesous* to the English *Jesus*. We could call him *Joshua Christ*.

Oh my *Joshua*.

I let loose a "Jesus Christ" in a circle of Christians recently and all their eyebrows raised. And I remembered, oh yes. There's a commandment about this, and in their eyes I just broke it.

"You shall not take the name of the Lord your God in vain."[2] I am not big on offending the Almighty, whom I doubt is easily offended anyway, but sometimes I need to call the people I love by both their first and last names when I want their attention. Jesus Christ, are you listening to me right now?

I search for a definition of "in vain" and come up empty-handed, that is, *unsuccessful, without results.* In vain. Can you utter God's name in vain? Is it even possible if nothing is impossible with God?

"THANK YOU, MISTER LOUIE!"

At a Mexican restaurant in Louisville, Kentucky my husband and I waited for the check with a set of friends. When it finally came, my friend said, "They must be really religious—the check says, 'Thank you, Jesus.'"

"I think that's his name," my husband said. "*Hey-soos*. Not Jesus."

---

1. Rom 8:38–39.
2. Exod 20:7.

But why not thank Jesus? Why not? Why do we say instead "thank goodness?" or "oh my gosh?" Who is Gosh? When I mean to thank God, why shouldn't I just say "thank God?"

"MISTER LOUIE IS WATCHING, LOOK BUSY."

"Jesus Christ," I mutter, "oh God, oh God," at the latest televised atrocity. Just turn on CNN or Fox News or whatever other 24-hour reality horror show you prefer and you'll be saying it, too, if your heart be not hardened, if your ears can hear, if your eyes can see.

Even the One Whose Name Feels Like Sandpaper Against the Roof of My Mouth cried out, "My God, My God, why have you forsaken me?"[3] That's *abandoned, why have you abandoned me?* God Himself felt left to die without any clear intervention from God Himself, bearing insults and suffering, bearing the weight of oppression and violence and mercilessness the exact way we don't want Him to bear it. We want Him to turn into the Warrior God, the Vengeful God, the Mighty Smiter, we want Him to come down from the Cross and prove Himself to be the god we want him to be, not the *I AM THAT I AM.*

When Jonah goes to talk to Nineveh, he's pissed when they actually listen to him and repent—all he really wanted was for God to destroy them. "I knew that You are a gracious and compassionate God, slow to anger and abundant in lovingkindness, and one who relents concerning calamity. Therefore now, O Lord, please take my life from me, for death is better to me than life."[4] I'd rather die than have you put up with this shit anymore. Enough of your patience. Enough of your abundant grace. Enough of your mercy triumphing over justice.

The news cycle turns over and it's "breaking" yet again, another earthquake, another bomb, another gun, another dead boy whose face will only haunt our dreams for a little bit before we pass over him, because really, what else can we do but change the channel, say a prayer, maybe send a check to a nonprofit to feel better. "Vanity of vanities," says the most cynical Teacher in Ecclesiastes, "Vanity of vanities! All is vanity."[5]

Maybe every whispered prayer in times like these is vanity.

---

3. Mark 15:34.
4. Jonah 4:2-3.
5. Eccl 1:2.

"WHAT WOULD MISTER LOUIE DO?"

In the Old Testament, whenever God called out His people by name, they answered, "Here I am." Here we are on earth, you and me. I am here. *I AM THAT I AM* is here. Somehow we are now embedded with this Presence, this Love, to be here, to be present, to represent. There is a name above all names we keep saying without meaning, and I'm tired of it.

I'm tired of saying "Jesus" when we should be seeing "Hey-soos."

"Lord, when did we see You hungry, or thirsty, or a stranger, or naked, or sick, or in prison, and did not take care of You?"[6]

Mister Louie would see. Mister Louie would hear. Mister Louie would sit bedside. Mister Louie would act. Mister Louie would show up. Mister Louie would offer His lunch. Mister Louie would wait. Mister Louie would be kind. Mister Louie would save.

"MISTER LOUIE HAVE MERCY."

My best friend's fiancé's mom died suddenly of pneumonia two months before their wedding. "Oh God, I'm so sorry," I text. There are no other words here, though others will surely be delivered about "more angels needed in heaven" or worse, "her time to go." Lord have mercy on us, who claim to be salt of the earth and instead sprinkle salt in wounds.

When Brian Doyle was diagnosed with brain cancer, a friend set up a GoFundMe account and donations came from everywhere. I believe it was God who moved through him to move others to love him, who seemed to love everyone and everything that the Lord God made and called good. It was the perfect 21st-century triune, the blessing we give and take and give and take, a giant, virtual, tangible, incarnate communion of saints.

And then he wasn't healed. And then he died. It is both horrible and holy how things break and heal and die and live forever.

My best friend has written in permanent ink in her skin, *Kyrie Eleison*, which translates to "Lord have mercy." Lord have mercy. Lord of that Name, that bloodied, beaten, tortured Name pinned to a Cross that some claim was placed there to appease an angry father. Lord have mercy, compassionate and gracious God. Lord of heaven, Lord of earth, Lord of the weary, Lord of the worn, Lord of the poor, Lord of the beaten, Lord of the peacemakers, Lord of the lost, Lord of the broken. Lord who saves. Lord have mercy.

---

6. Matt 25:44.

The Lord's Name

"MISTER LOUIE SAVES."

From a bridge today an Amish man in a straw hat and black pants signaled down to the semi I passed. *Honk your horn!* He pulled his imaginary air-horn string, the one I know hangs slack above the driver's left shoulder, and wouldn't you know it, the driver obliged, two long *blats* like a tuba's. The Amish man's signal turned into a wave and then we were all gone, the bridge, the road, the parallel lanes, the Amish man, the semi-truck driver I passed, and me.

We were gone, another communion of saints concluded.

I want to tell you how full the world is with joy and Brian Doyle-isms and semi-truck drivers and Amish men on bridges, but I'm afraid of waxing sentimental in the midst of all this cynicism and sadness ("everything is vanity, everything is meaningless"), though who wouldn't want a sentimental wax? I'll take a little dab of that. I want to keep feeling it roll against my ribcage from the inside.

There are so many bridges that end other than in two long air-horn blats of interaction. There are so many other bridges that separate us, body from spirit, flesh from bone, son from mother, real life from a screen. There are fallen bridges, jumped bridges, and broken bridges. We could have just missed it, just not been paying attention. There ought to be more air-horns sounded just for the joy of the thing. There ought to be more signals, more connections, more hands raised not for protection but in presence, in preservation, in praise.

Here I am, here I am, here I AM.

"DON'T TAKE MISTER LOUIE'S NAME IN VAIN."

Maybe the commandment means something more than what we've made of it, like so many commandments passed from priest to parishioner that have lost the heart and kept the hammer. Maybe God never meant the command to be about what we say but what we do—whose name we do it in. If God is love, then the commandment becomes *do not take love in vain, do not make love in vain, do not say you love and not mean it or do it or give it legs or make it move*, do not be a clanging cymbal or a banging gong, do not say *Lord, Lord* or *Jesus, Jesus*, and never feed the hungry, never clothe the naked, never tend to the widow or the orphan. Do not say love and then hate. Do not say love and then walk away. Do not wait for God to move when God is love and you could be loving and moving right this minute, loving and moving in love with your loved ones and your unloved ones, making good neighbors instead of good fences, building Amish-air-horn bridges instead of bigger bombs.

Maybe if we just give this a try for a bit, I can get over this name thing and just follow Mister Louie, like he said.

One day Elizabeth said something so naked and direct about Mister Louie that after she said it I excused myself and walked out of the room and wrote it down. "It doesn't matter what we call him," she said. "It doesn't matter what his name is really. It just matters that we can still talk to him and that he said love is the boss. Isn't that right?"[7]

—Brian Doyle

---

7. Doyle, "Mister Louie," *Leaping: Revelations and Epiphanies*, 52.

Underwater

Save me, O God, for the waters have threatened my life.
—Psalm 69:1

"Don't jump into the pool."
The words echo off of the pike, eels, and starfish painted on the cinderblock, animals that are born in the water, breathe underwater, survive and thrive underwater. All of the boys and girls in my children's swim class shed their swim belts and noodles and begin cleaning up, shivering and purple-lipped after forty-five minutes in the water. The air in the pool is stifling. I grab the kids' towels while balancing my six-month-old baby, Henry, on my left hip, ready to escape the chlorinated air, my head throbbing with chemicals.

"Don't jump into the pool," the swim instructor warns, and as she turns her back to help another swimmer out of the water, I watch my four-year-old, brave after swimming across the pool twice, courageous after jumping in with his blue sponge belt cinched tightly around his waist during his second swimming lesson, daring after forty-five minutes of safe interaction with water, jump into the pool.

"Turn around, turn around, turn around, turn around!" I'm saying to the instructor, to myself, in my head, out loud, walking as quickly as I can with Henry on my hip, wanting to run, to dive, to rescue my son who is drowning right before my eyes, to lift the little body kicking and paddling as hard as he can the way he was taught during the lesson, to raise the head I cupped in my hands when he was a newborn, the head that is now bobbing just underneath the surface, so he can inhale that glorious oxygen I don't even have to think about here on the solid concrete floor. Henry is tucked close between my chest and my left arm, our beach towels and my purse in my right arm, and I don't know what to do, I don't know—how do I jump into the pool with Henry? *Reach out, you are a foot away from the side of the pool!* Why won't my vocal chords shout it out, *Turn around!*, the swim instructor is right there, *right behind you*, and that little body just keeps kicking and pushing, fighting to the surface and failing, failing.

It takes only five seconds and I am there by the side of the pool. The swim instructor has pulled him out and sat him down on the edge of the water. He is sobbing but breathing, thank God. He didn't inhale any water; he must have held his breath. He is scared and I crouch down, hold him, hear his crying and breathing, yes, breathing, loving the way he's breathing even though he's shaking and just one second ago he was there, under the water, battling with everything he had to just break the surface. I want to yell, *Why didn't you listen?! Why do you have to test and disobey?! Do you see now? Do you see how dangerous this world is and why we ask you to follow the rules? Do you see?* But all he needs from me right now is warmth, to kiss his wet head and hold his shivering, sobbing body, his body that is alive and breathing and operating just as it should.

※

This day could have turned out much different, I think to myself in moments like this, replay what happened and rewrite the ending—water in the lungs, limbs slowing their movements, sinking, pulling a limp child, my child, cold and dripping and lifeless, from the pool and then pumping his chest, breathing air back into his lungs, but nothing. *Nothing.* And then what? Can I imagine the next sentence? It isn't possible to consider what this life might be like without a child we have conceived in it. I can't make the jump.

Every time he goes under, every time he chokes on his water at the kitchen table, every time he inhales water in the tub and gags, water down the wrong tube, water up his nose, water in his face, I remember his first days. When they pulled Elvis from my womb in that operating room and he screamed and everyone cheered because *Elvis has entered the building!* one nurse knew there was something not quite right about that yell, that thirty-nine-week, full-term baby's yell, that cry that meant no air was coming in unless he was screaming, unless he was fighting for it, sucking air like trying to breathe through a snorkel in the ocean during a hurricane.

The nurse saw the struggle and it wasn't good. She pulled him up. What if she only thought *this is a cranky one* and bundled him up in a swaddling blanket, respiratory distress syndrome slowly suffocating him?

※

Elvis is trying to muffle his crying on the edge of the pool. In the echo chamber of this humid and chlorinated room, I hear the eerie silence of twenty babies not crying and the good beeps of heart rates and the bad beeps of low oxygen levels. I feel the weight of my motionless newborn intubated in his Isolette, his full-term body heavy in my hands as the nurse changes his blanket, the constant beeping and monitoring, oxygen levels rising and dropping, and the prayers. *Just let the air come. Let the lungs expand on their own like they are supposed to when you are born on time.* Even in those early days he fought, against his lungs, against the breathing tube, against death, wrestled with angels and breathing machines, CPAP and surfactant until the oxygen levels rose, until finally he was well. He is fighting still, strong-willed and stubborn and brave. *Don't jump into the pool.*

That day could have turned out a lot different.

※

I fell in once. Visiting my great-grandmother, off an inflatable raft in a neighbor's pool. I dangled my legs over the edge, kicked around until the raft and my suit were wet. In my memory, I watch myself slip off and fall underneath the surface, drift to the bottom to sit cross-legged and wait for someone to notice I am gone. The water was cool and quiet, voices muffled. I don't remember the lifting, just the falling, holding my breath, waiting, waiting, waiting.

But I am a great swimmer now; my mom was a lifeguard as a teenager and taught my brothers and me to swim. Dad "helped" by throwing us into the pool, our bodies tucked tight in a cannonball or limbs flailing and smacking hard against the water. I will front crawl or breaststroke in any body of water, salt or fresh, sand or silt bottom, indoor or outdoor. I love to push beyond the breaking waves where the water rolls in steady lunges, where my feet can't touch, float over the surface, the current carrying me down the coastline a ways as I stare up into the cloudless blue until my temperature cools and I begin to shiver and prune, delighted to see how far I've been taken from my blanket on the shore. I've only lived close enough to the ocean for four months during college, but long enough to learn how to swim in the depths, dive in a wetsuit, kick with flippers, monitor my oxygen tank, adjust a buoyancy vest, and breathe using scuba gear underwater like it's normal to do that kind of thing. It's been ten years since I went scuba diving, but I remember the thrill of hovering under the surface, the way the water caught and stunned the sunlight, the way the beams electrified the coral reef, the way I felt weightless, beautiful, delicate. Being underwater made me feel holy.

As kids, we used to challenge each other to see who could stay under the longest. We closed our eyes, took a deep breath, and then pushed ourselves to the bottom. And it was a push too; you really had to force yourself to stay under, propelling the water heavenward with your hands as if to encourage a crowd to stand up and applaud. Strange, when you want to sink, you float; when you want to float, you sink. *Twenty-seven, twenty-eight, twenty-nine . . .* and then you surface, gasping and spitting and wiping the water from your face. "How long? How long? I bet I can stay under longer next time."

We jumped with abandon into any in-ground or above-ground pool, stepped wildly into the muddy banks of creeks and ponds—slime oozing between our toes—tried to body surf the waves in Lake Erie or the Atlantic Ocean on vacations, shaking sand out of our suits when the ocean got the best of us. Mom would cup her hands around her mouth and shout, "You are out too far!" but it was no big deal to us. We could touch.

꽃

Standing on the shore of Lake Erie at East Harbor State Park the summer before the swim lessons start, where the water in the designated swimming area reaches up to my knees at its deepest, I understand my mother's panic and the frantic waving for our attention.

Elvis and Lydia, four and five years old, flit about in the water lapping the shore. There are hundreds of people at the beach today, and my two children seem to shrink in size with every yard they go out. A motorboat passes, kicking up waves that ignore the breakwall and roll in relentlessly, threatening to knock over my suddenly small and unsteady children. Every muscle in me twinges. I experience several minor heart attacks as they falter against this frightening, gleeful power that is refreshing and deadly, life-giving and life-taking away. I jump off of the towel and stride toward the water, making a megaphone out of my hands.

"Come back toward the shore! You are out too far!" I yell to the tiny bodies I know are my children by the way the sunlight bounces off their skin as they wiggle in the water. *But what's the big deal, Mom, it's only waist-deep on us, and can't you see we're invincible?* I cross my arms against my damp swimsuit, my bare feet sinking in the muddy sand.

✻

Elvis cries the entire next swim lesson. No, he sobs. He screams. After thirty minutes in the pool, his hair is still dry. When the instructor asks him to jump in (with his floatation device on), he runs away, shivering and hiccuping. I try to bribe him with lunch at McDonald's, I try to reason with him about why he needs to learn to swim, I try to encourage him to be brave, I try to shower him with praise from the sidelines, but still he cries, even as he kicks and paddles his way across the pool, his neck muscles tense, his jaw jutting forward, every movement concentrating on keeping his head above the water. His tears fall freely, and then finally the lesson is over. We don't go back.

He is afraid. It is impossible to explain to him in a way that will make sense that if he listens and obeys the people who know what is good and right for him, this will turn out well; he'll learn how to swim, and it will be fun. But if he steps outside of those boundaries, well, the water is dark, menacing, and dangerous. He might get lucky, or he might not. There are words I can use to say these things, but he cannot hear them. All he hears is his own panic at being underwater without any way to breathe. He feels the water gripping his throat and pulling him under. I feel it, too. I'd rather not go back, either.

In the baptismal service at our church, the public confession of faith involves stepping into a large tub of warm water and allowing the pastor to push you under. You cross your arms in front of you and hold your nose, and he supports your body like he's going to show you how to float, one arm on your back and the other on your crossed arms, but then instead of keeping you above the surface, he lowers you under, so far under that your whole body is immersed in the Father and the Son and the Holy Spirit. That's the fear of learning to float—you have to trust that the person holding you up isn't going to let you sink. That the water is going to support your land-lubber body. Or, that someone else is going to bring you back up before it's too late.

In short, you have to let go. There is fear and obedience, faith and surrender.

And it's just a bathtub of water.

Elvis and Lydia are pretending to swim in the bathtub upstairs. They are squealing and laughing and inevitably, Elvis inhales the bathwater, jerks upright and gags until the water comes back out his nose and his mouth. He seems surprised that this has happened—even though it happens every single time—as if he expected to sprout gills between the last bath and this one. Still, my imagination sings its horrible song, Odysseus's siren that carries me from this ordinary evening of splashing and laughter to emergency rooms, intensive care units, heart monitors and breathing machines, redlines and long beeps and then, and then . . .

This is the wretched song, the what-ifs, the close calls, the ball bouncing out into a busy street, the car that missed the stop sign, the lifeguard who didn't turn around in time, the wave that knocked the toddler over, the mom who couldn't spot her daughter in the water among all the others, the mom who went downstairs to change a load of laundry while her children were bathing. Fear, fear rolling in waves, stifling, paralyzing fear, and worry, knuckle-biting, hand-wringing, teeth-clenching worry. This day, every day, every painful second, could have turned out much different. Every neck muscle tensed in resistance—*I will not surrender! You will not pull me under!* That is fear: relentless, exhausting, overwhelming, suffocating.

In the Gospels, Peter was called out of his boat by Jesus to walk to Him on the water, but when he saw the waves, he started to sink. Jesus reached him and pulled him up, scolded and comforted like a mother, "You of little faith, why did you doubt?"[1] What a strange question. Why? Because there were waves. Because it was water—deadly, powerful, dark water—because it is out of my control, bigger than me, all-consuming. Because I will sink below the surface and drown.

Because my kids will sink below the surface and drown. Because to be called out onto the water and to be expected to walk with faith, knowing the properties of water and the odds that I will die, he will die, we will die, they will die, one way or the other, today or tomorrow or eighty years from now, die by drowning, fluid filling our lungs, hearts wrenching, oxygen cut off from the brain, kidneys failing, blood slowing, consciousness swishing,

---

1. Matt 14:31.

humming, buzzing away. Death is waiting under the water, and you want me to walk on it. You want me to believe and not to doubt that someone will notice that I'm drowning and pull me up.

But they might not, and you want me to have faith, anyway, beyond the dying, beyond the cresting of the waves, the bobbing in and under the surface, the echo chamber of the pool, the uncertainty and certainty of this. You want me to get beyond this fear.

Last summer before the swim lessons started, Lydia, Elvis, and I walked in the water together at East Harbor State Park, all of us laughing, my children looking up at me and me looking down at them as we walked back toward the beach together. After calling from the shore, I joined their splashing and laughing, lifted their agile bodies out of the water and spun them around. We walked into the deeper waters where they couldn't go alone, and I held them up. It was one of the first times I could really play with them since the birth of Henry. On the way back toward our beach blanket, the kids got down on their bellies and "swam" in the shin-deep water—crawling like crabs all the way through the sand. Sometimes that is where it must begin, in the shallowest end of the lake, where walking on water is as easy as taking just one step.

The hotel we stayed at on vacation this spring, after our failed swim lessons, had an indoor pool. The five of us put on our swimsuits, rode the elevator down to the lobby, and entered the glassed-in pool area. Elvis hesitated on the first step, testing the water with his foot as he moved into it, stopping when the water came up to his waist. I swam over to him and put my hands on his waist, lifted him to my hip. He wrapped his legs and arms so tight around my body I could let go and still he didn't budge, but we eased in, spun around, and dipped up and down into the pool. I asked him if he wanted to jump in to me, my arms wide and ready, and he shook his head no, his body tensing. And that was okay. Someday, he will jump in with abandon, dipping under the water for a second until he bobs back up, hair and face soaked and shining, eyes blinking, a grin growing as he looks for me on the perimeter and waves, those little feet and arms paddling furiously below the surface.

15

YEAR ONE:

Fall 2003: Love Languages

"What makes you feel loved?" I asked. I knew the answer for me—spend time with me, walk with me, sit with me on the couch, play Scrabble with me, focus on me. And touch me. And tell me I'm beautiful and smart and capable. And maybe sometimes buy me things. Love me love me love me. At twenty-one I was a sponge for it, wanted all the love in the world, needed to know I was loved, needed to feel loved, unsure about whether I was worthy of love.

    Brandon squirmed next to me. It was night. We still measured the length of our marriage in weeks. This marriage devotional was my idea. "I don't know. When you do things for me, I guess," he said.

    "Do things? Like what kinds of things?" I asked.

    "Like, when you pack my lunch for me," he said.

    "Pack your lunch?" I laughed. "That's how you feel loved?"

    "This is stupid," Brandon said, rolling over and turning out the lights.

Summer 2004: Loss

Eager to become a family of three, we waited to hear the promising rapid chug-chug that would give viability to my positive pregnancy test. There was no heartbeat on the monitor. The embryo that had been growing stopped three weeks earlier.

It shouldn't have been a warm, sunny day. There shouldn't have been birds singing when we walked out of the building. There shouldn't have been people everywhere going about their normal lives. We had walked into the obstetrician's office with French fries and an orange drink from McDonald's for me to ward off morning sickness. Now there was only weight. Mass. Cells.

Brandon embraced me next to my car. "I guess I'll go back to work now and tell Cathy," I mumbled into his shoulder.

He squeezed and grabbed my hands, pressed his forehead against mine. "Be strong and courageous," Brandon prayed. "Do not be afraid; do not be discouraged, for the Lord your God will be with you wherever you go."[1]

YEAR TWO:

Fall 2004: The Slowness of Grief

The first baby we conceived was a partial mole pregnancy. To make sure the cancerous cells of the embryo were discharged fully from my system and not developing further in my lungs, I went weekly for blood tests, then monthly, the doctor monitoring hCG levels until the hormone disappeared.

I stared out the passenger side window. Why did this happen? What did I do to deserve this loss? Why are others able to just get pregnant and I can't? What penance am I paying? Why did this happen? What if we never have a baby? Why did this happen? Tree after tree after tree after tree, light pole after light pole after light pole, mailbox, mailbox.

"You know, this is hard for me too," Brandon said, voice like lighthouse through the fog. I turned to look at the man who kept driving me forward, along the slow road.

Spring 2005: The Power of Distraction

The second baby we conceived was just a line on a pregnancy test before it failed too—too small to be seen on an ultrasound screen.

"I learned my lesson the first time!" I screamed, certain the first miscarriage was a test to learn empathy and I had passed. It felt unfair. God had promised the desires of our heart if we only delighted ourselves in Him.

1. Josh 1:9 (NIV).

Hadn't we delighted? Is God a God of love? What about all that stuff about having a plan for me? What about all that stuff about working all things for the good? How is this good? How can He begin to fulfill a promise and then retract it? What lesson is there here for me? Who are You anyway?

We worked together at a Christian high school, and in the spring we worked and worked, me planning and preparing for the school's auction, Brandon coaching baseball and teaching full-time. I lost the romance of God's great wooing and sought a new foundation of truths I could stand on: Jesus wept. God so loved the world that he gave His only Son. His only Son cried Abba, Abba, why have you forsaken me? His only Son waited until after His best friend died to raise him again. His only Son suffered. And there was Resurrection. And there was new life. Nothing can separate us from the love of Christ, we learned, neither death nor life.

YEAR THREE:

Spring 2006: Abundance

The third baby we conceived gave me heartburn like you wouldn't believe and wanted to arrive twelve weeks early. To keep the contractions from coming, I went on modified bed rest, which basically meant I could lounge around the house and watch TV or read but I couldn't do laundry, or cook, or clean.

It was rough.

The meals from families at our school arrived every other day—salads and rolls, entrees and sides, always a potato and always a dessert—enough to feed a family of five. Love came baked and steamed and tossed and creamed, sometimes so delectable we asked for the recipes, with the occasional flop we felt guilty not eating.

One Sunday in church, our daughter rolled from one side of my abdomen to the other, back and forth, her cantaloupe-sized body trying to get comfortable, maybe excited by the cinnamon-sugar bagel I ate that morning. I squeezed Brandon's hand and stopped listening to Pastor Coffey talking. We watched the magnificence of movement, the results of cells coming together and binding, staying together, growing, deciding which ought to be an eye and which ought to be a toe, cells committed to growing a beating heart, breathing lungs, limbs to kick and punch, all growing, growing, miraculous and ours, hidden by my own skin. She shifted once and twice and again a third time, and we watched the bump distort from left to right and back, almost there, almost born, almost done, almost ready but not yet, not yet.

Summer 2006: How We're Wired

All my life I thought I'd be exactly like my mom when I grew up. There aren't many women in my world I admire more, and Mom was the stay-at-home variety, for the most part. She served as the behind-the-scenes engine of my parents' business, paying bills and processing paperwork, handling the finances of their excavating company while raising my brothers and me. She was ever and always there for me, so reliable I rarely appreciated her presence until after I left home.

Leading up to Lydia's birth, we calculated the costs of staying home with her because of course I would; it was what I'd always wanted to do. Maybe I could work part-time here and there, but of course I'd be at home. I'd take her to the zoo with her cousins; we'd read books and take walks and naps and make meals and crafts and it would be glorious.

And then she arrived, beautiful and sleepy. I lost routine beyond feedings. I read her all of *The Chronicles of Narnia* while she nursed. I left half my brain in the hospital, felt disconnected and separate in conversations with nothing to say except how happy Lydia's sleep patterns made me. Who the heck would I be if I wasn't a stay-at-home mom? I called my boss and asked for my job back. Lydia came to work with me, and whatever had dimmed in my engine relit.

YEAR FOUR:

2006–2007: Miracles

When we found out about Elvis, Lydia was six months old and we weren't even trying to get pregnant (except we were doing everything you'd normally do to get pregnant). Apparently sometimes it really does just happen. Being pregnant with him was so easy, I sometimes forgot I was growing a person inside me. And besides, there was Lydia to chase after, Lydia to dote on and dress and show off to the world, her mom and dad's delight.

While I wasn't even thinking about being pregnant in the spring of 2007, we applied to jobs and seminaries around the nation, casting our nets in the direction of some calling. We believed that God had a plan for us beyond where we were at and considered stepping out on faith to make a move for seminary without the financial security of any paying jobs, but then an opportunity opened at my alma mater. Which happened to also have a seminary. In the same state where we lived already. Paying more than our combined salaries just for one of us.

Everything fell into place. I started my new job at Ashland in July, coordinated the first two-week-long summer residency for the graduate creative writing program, and worked until the day of my scheduled C-section.

Elvis was born at 9:40 a.m. with respiratory distress syndrome and pulmonary hypertension, a full-term baby who couldn't breathe through his underdeveloped lungs. They transferred him to Akron Children's sometime in the hazy twenty-four hours after my surgery, intubated and sedated, his situation so tenuous we couldn't touch him before he left us. In the rows of NICU infants ordered by severity of condition he was in bed #1. We waited and prayed for miracles both medical and spiritual.

On the road from home to hospital, I heard a song and felt a peace descend—whatever happens, it will be okay. It will be okay, whatever happens. No matter what? No matter what.

I held motionless Elvis in his incubator while the nurse changed his linens. I rubbed my scent into a cloth we placed next to his face. We watched the machines breathe for him, watched the monitors beep, watched as slowly he came back to life, and then suddenly he was in our arms, suddenly no longer fragile, suddenly strong and strong-willed and stubborn and *alive*.

YEAR FIVE:

Fall 2007: Limits

We moved to Ashland the last weekend of October, just as every family in town tucked away their yard furniture and pets to begin their winter hibernation. After being a full-time teacher and three-season high school coach, Brandon found himself stranded on Morgan Avenue, watching Sesame Street and Sports Center, folding laundry, making dinner, changing two sets of diapers, and supervising potty training. They became regulars at Walmart and Home Depot, wandering the aisles for something to do outside of the house.

15

My routine was the same each day—wake up, shower, put on dress pants and a blouse, apply makeup, blow-dry my hair, and come down the stairs for breakfast and a mug of tea before walking to work. I rounded the corner to Elvis and Lydia sitting at the kitchen table waiting for breakfast. Brandon wore black sleeping pants and a T-shirt. My heels clacked on the linoleum as I crossed the kitchen. I added several heaping spoonfuls of sugar to the steaming mug of tea. Brandon was silent.

"Well, I'm off to work," I said brightly.

Brandon slammed a kitchen cabinet shut and yelled, "I hate my life!"

I stared at him. Lydia sat at the table, Elvis sat in his high chair, our redbone coonhound, Tex, lounged in the living room. I loved this town. I loved our family. I loved my job. How was it possible for him to hate this life?

I left, tossing, "See you at lunch" over my shoulder and balancing my notebook and mug with one hand to open the back door. If he's so miserable, I mumbled to myself a dozen times that winter, why doesn't he just leave.

Spring 2008: The Value of Community

We had romanticized the notion of living in a college town: developing lasting friendships fast, hanging out with other administrators from the university, attending all the sporting events, and generally entering into the depth of community quickly—the type of bonds we'd left behind at Lake Center, where people genuinely cared what was happening in your life, beyond the workday.

Instead, most of my work interactions were conducted by email. The people I saw regularly were at least a generation older than us, their children grown and out of the house. If we wanted to make friends, we'd have to go after them.

It was hard to relate to the growing depression and anger Brandon felt about our circumstances in contrast to the bright delight of my own job and life satisfaction. I had everything I never could have hoped to want. He was doing nothing he ever dreamed of doing. We were the kind of alone made more distinct because we were together. If we wanted to stay together, we'd have to find others like us.

We walked into the church on campus one Sunday morning and left with two invitations to join a small group—not in an over-eager recruiter manner, just warmth, just join us. The sun came out. Winter thawed. People brought out their lawn furniture and pets again.

YEAR SIX:

2008–2009: The Value of Tradition (and Repetition)

What do you do when your kids are one and two? You walk to the park every sunny day. You eat breakfast and snack and lunch and nap and snack and dinner and bathe and read and sleep. You develop the names we'll call our grandparents and practice giving words and phrases meaning, inventing "Pop-Pop" and "Great Mom-O" and "chidewalk." With some of the darkness behind us, we delighted in the monotony, were aware of moments paused with child tucked into the crook of an arm, child standing on a stump, child sitting on a Dora couch, child licking brownie batter off a spoon.

Weekends were marked by memory making. For two people who did not possess the cognitive development to have memories of this season, we picked out pumpkins. We wrapped presents that would launch our family's Christmas traditions. We visited the zoo and winter festivals. We went sledding. We made snowmen.

No one suspects that when you go to the county fair with your kids once, it will become one of the many things you always do: we always go to the fair; we always eat pizza on Fridays; we always go to Topsail Beach.

It took all of our time and energy, this thing called parenting. We accidentally got pregnant on the pill and miscarried, again, this time a little relieved, a little guilty to be relieved. When the children were asleep, we played an occasional game of Scrabble. We watched a lot of shows, zombified and shell-shocked by the sheer constant noise and busyness of toddlers. We sometimes sat together on the couch and sometimes sat in separate spots. We sometimes rubbed the other's foot with ours and asked, "Are you ready for bed?" We sometimes saw friends who didn't have kids or whose children were past this age—we snuck them into our house after the kids were asleep or met them out at bars for karaoke—and some of them never saw us with our children at all. They were surprised to meet Parent Sarah and Parent Brandon—Friend Sarah and Friend Brandon our fly-by-night secret identities, the people we really were when we weren't trying to keep our children from killing themselves.

15

We did not possess the cognitive ability to know the work that was being done when our kids were two and one, but in these early, routine days, we were creating the culture of our family. We were binding them in security. We were giving them predictability. We were weaving together a safety net they could trust would be there whenever they fell.

YEAR SEVEN:

2009–2010: Friendship

After I worked the MFA program's summer residency in August, 2010, I went to the doctor to find the heartbeat of our sixth pregnancy and found none, again, and this time the sadness was buried in a dogpile of toddler and preschooler on top of me. Lydia was four and Elvis would turn three any day, and I was twenty-eight and we had been married a full seven years and life has been hard and surprising and full of joy and delight and sometimes deeply lonely even in the presence of many. We held each other and questioned whether to ever try to get pregnant again.

    I dropped the children in Sunday School and stood in the pew after the D&C that week. There were so many days where we were apart on Sundays, I can't remember now if you were there, too, husband, or if you were on your way home from some foreign city, working for ESPN again that weekend. As the band sang "Blessed Be the Name," I shuddered with grief I didn't expect my body to feel, and Jillian and LeeAnn were there, strength and comfort and presence in my thin space, my fragile space.

    On Friday nights after the children slept, I invited these women over for wine and chocolate and cheese. We'd watch a movie, or sometimes we would just sit and talk and laugh. On Friday nights, you were with a crew of people who would become your weekend friends from other cities, men who will sustain you in this season on the road. We were learning what it meant to parent together, separately. We were learning what it meant to be married half the week and single the other half and how to stay married in the midst of it, and the men and women who stood with us were a kind of fortress, a kind of shelter, a kind of shield.

Ordinary Time

YEAR EIGHT:

2010–2011: Delight

The seventh time we got pregnant would be the last, whether it stuck or not, and this one did. Every moment of this pregnancy was treasure. This was the last time in my life I would carry the promise of a child, feel the interior pressure of kicks and movement, use my belly as a TV tray. Pregnant with this final child, I felt holy.

When Henry came, it was the easiest gift of a birthing experience possible. We took the extra day in the hospital just to be together, me and him. Having Henry was a family affair—Lydia and Elvis were five and turning four when he was born—and everyone doted on this chubby one, this final addition that completed our immediate circle. He was a child born of love, born into a house of love, nurtured and adored.

We'd raise Henry unlike the other two, and he really would grow up in a different home. All that summer and into the fall we were a family unit. We were together in our small town, on maternity leave, barbecuing with friends, visiting extended family, going to Lydia's soccer and T-ball games, wearing Henry in a Baby Bjorn and later a backpack. Being right down the street from work, Brandon brought Henry into my office to nurse, and for a full year he never took a bottle. Something was different here. We knew how to do this now. We'd gotten this. And it was good.

YEAR NINE:

January 2012: Nutrition

Rescued by the saving grace of the Whole 30, Brandon and I became food evangelists. If eighteen-year-old fresh convert Sarah was obnoxious with her "everybody gets a Bible for Christmas" evangelizing, twenty-nine-year-old Paleo diet Sarah challenged her to laps around the dining room table.

But cutting out dairy, cheese, sugar, and grains made such a difference immediately for our overall health and well-being, how couldn't we tell everyone what happened to us? Besides weight loss, the digestive changes, the sinus changes, the sleep changes, the allergy reductions, the elimination of prescriptions . . . it felt like a miracle.

It was also the first thing since our children that we'd rallied around together, hard. We were in this, and we were in this deep. No more casseroles!

15

No more dessert! No more cream-of-anything! What interesting new food combination could we try tonight? Have you had these carrots?! These carrots are amazing! We felt terrific. We'd lost weight. There would not be another pregnancy here. After running a half-marathon in December and then adding nutrition in, I felt lean and near the size and dimensions I was when we first married, and Brandon looked, I'll just come right out and say it, hot. We are soon-to-be thirty and soon-to-be thirty-five, feeling attractive and thin and healthy and powerful and alive.

June 2012: Retreat

The place we went for our 9th wedding anniversary (and Valentine's Day, and our combined birthdays) was a six-and-a-half hour ride into the mountains of West Virginia, to Lost River. We lost the signal on our cell phones ten miles from the B&B but somehow managed to find it without GPS. After another full year of work and travel for work, we were in the blessed summer months where Brandon's work slowed down and I switched to summer hours.

There were no children with us. It was just us.

The B&B was in a valley. Across the road were rolls of hay bales scattered at random, golden against the green of a mountain. We walked from the B&B to the adjacent restaurant for an early dinner.

"Just so you know, I'm married," Brandon said to me, flashing his ring. "That's the first thing I say to women when I'm on the road." We laughed. It would be so easy to slip off the ring he held up for their inspection.

"The trouble is," I told him, "I prefer to talk to men." And he said between bites, "I know exactly what you mean. I enjoy talking to women." We left the restaurant holding hands, turned on James Taylor, slipped into the bed at the B&B and kicked off the sheets, broad daylight flitting through the blinds.

Everything seemed so amazing with us, right then. We were totally hot, mountaintop high in love, a perfect family of five with maybe its own little rocky roads, its pockets of loneliness, its moments of disappointment and disagreement, but deeply in love and grateful for what seemed like heaven there in Lost River, lost and away and being found by each other. There were storm clouds on the horizon, but we escaped them, that weekend; they were held back by the mountains, they were hedged in, and we were there.

Ordinary Time

YEAR TEN:

Fall 2012: Why We Make Vows

Here is one thing I learned in the fall of 2012: there are some people in the world who don't care about your marriage vows.

Here is another thing I learned in the fall of 2012: I do.

There is tension, temptation, strength, and fear between those two truths. Truth #1 makes me feel offended and flattered, violated and appalled. Truth #1 crept into my daily and evening routine with random texts and Facebook posts, and I was frantic with anxiety, trying to hold it all together—wanting to keep a work "friendship" while pushing away those sporadic flirtations, wanting the compliments to go away but also feeling noticed.

I threw myself into Truth #2: I do. There are Bible verses about temptation, and I wielded them like the sword the Word of God calls itself, aimed and stabbed, reminded myself over and over again but especially in the moments when marriage was less the "for better" and more the "for worse." Brandon was traveling again, and I went along for a weekend to retreat together. At home, our date nights took us golfing and to dinner, line dancing and out for drinks. Sometimes date night was Scrabble in the living room, sweet potato fries and guacamole and American Honey.

I didn't let on much to anyone what was happening. It was too much, and I am a woman who has things under control.

Spring 2013: Losing Control

Things started to fall apart. As a woman who has things under control, when those things start to push against the edges, the surface calm ruptures. Somewhere in the spring of 2013, after my mom's cancer diagnosis and Elvis's episode with kidney stones and more and more out-of-town travel trips, I officially lost it. I wanted to quit everything. I knew I was not alone, but I felt so alone. I didn't want to ask for help because I felt like I was always asking for help. I am stronger than this. I've got this.

It felt to me like Brandon was living his best life now, on the road with his road friends, traveling from city to city, eating at exotic restaurants, drinking bourbons. When he told me there was a new game on his schedule, I started to cry. "Look at me! This isn't me! I'm losing it! Why am I bawling right now?!"

That is what we do. We keep going.

Spring 2013: Mercies

On the day an essay I wrote got published, called "Field Guide to Resisting Temptation," Brandon went to a bar. There was a woman there he found attractive. We both knew already about this attraction. I teased him about her the first time we met her. This time, she came on to him. (Truth #1: there are some people in the world who don't care about your marriage vows.)

Brandon woke me up when he got home. "Your essay on temptation was published just today and then this happens," he said. "I understand, now, I understand." (Truth #2: we do.)

Summer 2013: What Parents Do after the Kids Go to Sleep When You're Camping

At Camp Sandusky, the children were asleep in our 10x10 shed. The crickets and the highway roared peacefully behind us. We watched the embers burn in the fire ring, played cards, drank sweet tea vodka. A lot of sweet tea vodka. There were so many ways we never imagined being here. Will this life always be this crazy? Are we missing it? Is this what we will do forever?

We cycle through these narratives every six months or so, in the quiet and undistracted minutes alone. Our marriage is not just tag-team grocery shopping and babysitting, laundry washed and folded, dinners discussed and cooked and eaten; no, we are creators and dreamers, lovers and friends, ambitious and insecure, weathering the seasons together as best as we can.

The fire dimmed and the night air cooled. I was grateful for our double seater, for darkness, for sweet tea vodka. We kissed. We did some other things. Camp Sandusky turned out to be not so bad after all.

YEAR ELEVEN:

Fall 2013: Landmark Occasions

Celebrating ten years together felt like circling around for a victory lap. Whew! We made it! Nothing seemed impossible now. We traveled together to Blacksburg, Virginia. Brandon's gift to me that anniversary was a new engagement ring and an original song, and it felt like a brand-new promise, a renewed commitment to this crazy life.

Sometimes I think I'm too hard to love, maybe not worthy enough, and then I lean back and there is my husband, my best friend, the one person in the world I can be fully me around, the one person who knows all of this hot mess and loves anyway.

Ten years was big. Ten years was amazing. Ten years was a mountain range of memory, a topographical map of emotion and we were climbing out of a valley, standing on a summit looking back at what was, ready to turn toward what will soon be.

Winter 2013: Forgiveness and Priorities

We tell each other everything, now.

When human resources training about sexual harassment triggered a physical reaction in me, I texted Brandon with shaky hands and heart racing. *Oh. Oh, so that's what was happening. You mean I didn't have to put up with all of that nonsense? Why didn't anyone tell me, ever, that sometimes you don't have to be nice? Why didn't anyone tell me that sometimes being nice comes at the expense of something greater?* I was immediately angry instead of just ashamed, enraged, and embarrassed. After I came home and we finished the nightly routine, it was time for sweet potato fries and guacamole in the kitchen.

"I am so sorry, Brandon," I cried. "I'm so sorry, because I didn't know; I just didn't know what was happening." Our children slept soundly in their beds upstairs, fans roaring for white noise. The sliced sweet potatoes waited on the counter to be tossed with olive oil.

"Why are you apologizing?" he asked.

"Nothing happened, but all of that nothing wrecked an entire year. I hate how off my priorities were." Our eyes were locked, now, even from the distance across the kitchen. "I was so worried about preserving friendships, keeping silent so I didn't cause a scene, holding the status quo, being nice, that I failed to protect what is most important here. You. Us. Our family. What we've built. That is what kills me. I'm so sorry. I'm so sorry." I couldn't stop saying it, I'm so sorry.

Brandon looked down for a moment and then up again at me, "I forgive you, for whatever it is that you feel like you need to apologize for. I love you," and then the land masses we stood on collided. We held each other long in the kitchen, tears falling heavy on each other's shoulders, kissing the tears away, salt strong on our lips.

Summer 2014: Seasons

Summer is our season; this season is magical. We took a full ten-day trip to the Carolinas and to Florida, stopping to see friends and family along the way. Our little people were growing bigger. Disney and Sea World seemed like destinations we all left carrying home only the best memories. Maybe we brought our best selves with us. Maybe they were pumping more than the pleasant smell of cotton candy into the parks. Or maybe we were all just present for each other, and happy, and not working, and here—together.

YEAR TWELVE:

December 2014: Chocolate Cake and Humility

One thing I learned in December 2014: don't try to keep up with the guys who are drinking bourbon at your new job's end-of-year party and also eat chocolate cake the night before you're supposed to fly to Connecticut for a wedding.

You will recover before the wedding ceremony, but it'll take a solid twenty-four hours, after you've stumbled out of the Uber driven by a Russian immigrant, after you've mumbled "Dos-vee-dan-ya" to him and wobbled toward the first night away with your husband in months, after you don't quite make it to the toilet, after your husband mopped up your mess from the bourbon and chocolate cake, after you board a plane greener than you've ever been and feel as if you won't make it, but you make it, even begin to feel human again by the time you land.

You will recover, but everything about your life you will hate during this twenty-four-hour period of time.

Spring 2015: New Seasons

At Brandon's grandma's house, there was always something new blooming. I walked around the yard after working in Cleveland all day, dealing with rush hour traffic between Case Western Reserve and Akron, and admired all the flowers. There were so many varieties of perennials blooming there.

We went out together to dinner and a concert—Lyle Lovett and John Hiatt—and there were no children with us. We did our best not to talk about the children, to only talk about us, to have fun.

"Just think," Brandon said, "in three years we'll be able to leave Lydia with the boys and just, leave." I couldn't imagine it in that moment, that stage of life seemed so distant.

We were in a new neighborhood with new friends and new jobs, in a new house in a new school district away from our old community, closer to family. Everything was different, even living in Brandon's grandma's house. Everything needed to be made new.

The distance from Ashland and my old job was liberating in a way I didn't know I needed, so even though the days were long, and we didn't see as much of each other, we were together. John Hiatt was wailing, "Have a little faith in me," and we do.

YEAR THIRTEEN:

Fall 2015: Patience

The fall of 2015 began Donkey's Farewell Tour—Brandon's last season of working on the road with ESPN. When "Donkey" (Brandon's road nickname) was gone, he was out late eating great food and drinking lots of bourbon with friends (who nicknamed him). When Donkey was home, he was impatient, irritable, distant, and angry.

I walked a deserted Lake Michigan shoreline with a girlfriend on a writer's retreat in October, sifting through my discontent. I told her how scared it made me to not miss my husband when he left every weekend for work, how relieved I was when he was gone, how the air cleared and I could love and parent our children in peace, how much I hated that feeling, that feeling that we would be okay . . . maybe even better, if he left.

I started a lot of sentences with, "The worst thing is . . ." to describe the loneliness, the separation, the navigation of off-kilter schedules, the depression.

"The worst thing is," I said grayly, "it's like he doesn't even care anymore. Like he's tired of dealing with me and my neediness, like he's given up on trying. And that's worse than anything that's gone between us before."

What I failed to remember in the immediacy of my personal crisis was Brandon's own personal crisis: what would he be if he wasn't Donkey with

15

ESPN? What did the future hold on the other side of January? All I knew was I couldn't sustain another year alone, with Donkey.

In the chaos spinning between our separate-but-together personal crises, a whisper: *Just wait. See how things are in January. Just wait. Be patient. Love is patient.*

Winter 2015: Lament

The Thursday after the October Lake Michigan retreat, we learned Mom's kidney cancer was back, scarily back, stage IV back, and the neediness I felt in our marriage became eclipsed by treatment plans, hospital stays, and anticipatory grief. The day after Mom's diagnosis, Brandon encouraged me to get a dog, and then there was Izzy, the main character of my Instagram feed.

December meant more days in the hospital than out, and all I knew of my Advent traditions with our family shifted to lamentations. I wrote of the times God had been with us before, even in our deepest moments of despair, and how this backstory can encourage us in this current moment of despair. We clung to hope. We waited.

Still Winter, but 2016: Retreat, Again

In January, days after Donkey's final road trip with ESPN, we took a trip to Hocking Hills with some of our closest friends, without our children between us all the way.

I didn't know how it would go. I knew I would have fun with my girlfriends and I knew he would have fun with his guy friends, but what of the car ride south? What of any isolated time together? We would be together for two and a half days.

It had been too long. Sometimes you forget who the person across from you is and only see what that person does. Without the distractions and disagreements over how to parent our children, we are who we are, together.

It was January. The radio played bad Billy Joel songs and now any time there are dark clouds on the horizon, one of us says, "there's a storm front comin," and the other replies, "mood indigo."

Ordinary Time

YEAR FOURTEEN:

2016–2017: Wilderness

Every day we could, Brandon and I took walks around our neighborhood in Copley with Izzy. It was a one-mile trek. We left the kids at the house and walked. We walked and talked. We walked and didn't talk. We talked and laughed. We talked and disagreed and explained what made us angry and made jokes to break the tension and we walked. We walked and walked. We walked the same mile over and over and traveled farther, deeper, better, healthier. Eating and sleeping and drinking and walking. The circumstances of our lives shifted and we shifted too.

Brandon was around a lot more in the fall of 2016 and I started a new job in the winter of 2017, and we were both sorting out what all of this meant, wandering around the wilderness together, reforming our understanding of faith, rebuilding trust, searching for a new understanding of our identities.

Fourteen years ago, Brandon and I thought to ourselves, we could really nail this thing called marriage. We should go into marriage ministry! Neither of us knew what it meant to be equipped for marriage ministry.

To "minister" is to tend to the needs of someone else. We thought the way to practice marriage ministry was to turn outward from our marriage and inspect other couples, tell other couples what they should do to have the best marriage now.

But what we needed to do was turn inward, to learn how to tend to the needs of each other. To be married. To stay married. To practice marriage. To minister within our own marriage.

It turns out we've been practicing marriage ministry now for fourteen years and haven't sat with a single couple for premarital counseling. We haven't led a marriage retreat. We haven't served on staff at a church or set curriculum on sex and money and fidelity.

There's a Christian saying that marriage isn't meant to make you happy; it's meant to make you holy. I kind of hate that. Mostly because such one-liners are thrown out as if they contain all truth and that's it, there's nothing else to say. Obviously, if you are not happy in your marriage it's because that isn't what it's about; it's about holiness and that's the end of the conversation.

But what is holiness except the profound deepening and widening of our understanding of God's love for us? What is holiness except the experience of having your heart enlarged and beaten and restored, spurred on to love others more abundantly? What is holiness except the manifestation of the fruits of the Spirit?

And the fruits of the Spirit are first love, then joy, followed by peace, patience, kindness, goodness, faithfulness, gentleness, and self-control.[2] A marriage that is made holy has turned inward to each other's needs, and by doing so, refracts the Spirit outward. Love and joy. Holiness and happiness.

So we walk, and walk, and walk. And slowly, we are restored, from the inside out.

YEAR FIFTEEN:

Fall 2017: Settling

We bought what Brandon affectionately called our "death house"—forget the forever home business, this was the place we'd die someday. It was unlike any other house, with weird pockets of weirdness tucked into corners of weirdness. We loved it.

The place we bought was where we wanted to stay. Shedding the burden of "what's next" was a strange new relief for me. This was it. This was what we were doing. This right here. This was where we were going to be. Right here. This would be where our children would return when they are grown with their young children, return to visit us and Izzy, who will by then be the world's longest living dog because she will never die of course.

Every single step and turn earlier in our marriage came with a "what if" packaged with a "what next?" "When this is over," we would say, "we'll do something different, go somewhere else, lift up roots and transplant again into new soil or just rest awhile till we discern the next destination." And then off we went again.

But now, we were certain of what we hoped for. Certain. Returning to Ashland was many things, but what it marked in my heart was a firm renewal that we were here, together—this marriage—this love—this family—this world we were building together.

This was what I had been waiting for, this. This hope. This steady rise, this cup overflowing, this contentment, this open space, this peace, this faith, this rest, this firm ground.

And it was here now. It was here. Right here.

2. Gal 5:22-23.

Summer 2018: How We See the World

It was warm and sunny with a slight breeze on Punderson Lake when we decided to take our boys canoeing. We were camping, and Lydia was with her grandparents in Akron. Elvis and I paddled slowly on the water, gliding over the surface, alternating strokes on the left and the right. We glided near the lily pads and watched for signs of fish.

"This is so relaxing," I sighed. "Oh, look! A crane!" I pointed toward what I assumed was a great blue heron, because I loved the great blue heron. Blue, solitary, gawky . . . it was my spirit animal.

"This is exhausting," Brandon said.

Nearby, Henry and Brandon smacked the surface of the water with their oars. The wind was gusting. They kept getting tangled in seaweed. Henry wasn't paddling with any kind of regularity. It was a struggle.

We steered our canoes toward the opposite shore. I snapped a few pictures of Elvis in the bow of the boat and answered a call from my mom from the canoe. We paddled along some more.

"Oh no!" Splash. Elvis and I turned in the direction of Brandon and Henry who had just gone overboard into the water. The canoe righted itself, Henry bobbed in the water, and Brandon began swimming toward him.

Elvis could not stop laughing. He was laughing his head off. Laughing harder than maybe I'd ever heard him laugh. "Shhh, don't let Dad hear you laughing," I told Elvis as we paddled toward the overboard crew of our second ship.

I held the canoe steady. Brandon climbed back in. We helped Henry pull himself up on the edge of the canoe and back in the boat.

"Well," Henry said, "That was an experience."

I laughed. "Yes, that was an experience. I bet you're cooled off now!"

Brandon was certain they had almost drowned. "That's the last time I'm ever going canoeing."

"Oh, it was fun!" I said.

I am the silver lining to Brandon's storm clouds. He is the reality check in my fantasy land. Some days, it drives us nuts about each other. Other times, it's our saving grace.

Skipping Stones

I AM standing with my children in the bed of river rocks that have been broken and smoothed to flat disks, millennia wearing away the rough places. My daughter gathers stones and skips them along the shallow surface. As I dip my hand into the river to retrieve a couple pebbles, I see the stones I wear on my left ring finger glistening in the creek. They are new and old, ancient in their creation and recently purchased by my husband of ten years. Five are on my wedding band—diamonds I deemed "stones of remembrance" after we married. Stones like the Israelites carried through and across the Jordan, stones the children could see later and ask, "What do these stones mean?" Back then, I thought, *Faith. Hope. Love.*

It has been a decade. Now, the new engagement ring he purchased to replace the cubic zirconium look-alike shines with other meaning. These days, I say yes, faith, yes, hope, yes, love, but also grace, mercy, redemption, the way the river's rushing floodwaters polish the ragged edges, the way that liquid smooths granite—the way you can hold something so dense in your hand and with a gentle flick of the wrist cast it away to either sink with a plunk to the bottom, or to dance and skip across the water, touching the surface for a single second then lifting again, a train of ripples spreading out behind.

Little Joys: Neural Intimacy

"THE answer is always yes."

This is the latest rule of life in the Wells marriage. And yes, the first marriage thing you thought of is on the list, along with hot tea, nachos, and bourbon. There is no reason to ask whether the other of us wants tea, or nachos, or bourbon, or sex, the answer is always yes.

It's said that when a couple has spent a long time together, they start to look and sound like each other. It's actually true, because, science. But it's also true that people begin to think like each other. In his book *Powers of Two*, Joshua Wolf Shenk sees the connectivity between couples as a shared mind that allows them to be more creative together than they would be on their own.

Our different ways of processing the world rubs off on each other; it sharpens the dull edges of our perspectives until we are no longer exactly like the person we were when we first met. We see things differently, collectively.

We share a mind, not in a direct replica of the other person, but in cognitive, experiential proximity, holding another person's thoughts and emotions with the same love and concern, as closely as our own. There's actually a psychological term for this, *neuro-intimacy*, which is essentially what I'm talking about here: that deep connection you have with a person that allows you to let down your guard and be exactly who you are, share exactly what you think, because the degree of trust between you is so strong.

You know what the other person is going to say before they say it. You remember the same memory simultaneously. You say the same thing at the same time, glance at one another and grin. *He gets me.*

Little Joys: Neural Intimacy

"No man is an island entire of itself" wrote John Donne.[1] We are interwoven, the ever-expanding patchwork quilt of our lives growing more complex and connected the longer we are together.

Brandon and I have known each other for twenty years and will celebrate our 20th wedding anniversary next September. When you've been in contact with someone daily for 7,300 days the way we have, you've had 7,300 opportunities to develop neural intimacy.

It isn't just true of romantic relationships or marriages, but of friendships, sibling bonds, the connection between a parent and her child. We develop our own private languages and our own inside jokes, and we say exactly what we mean to say from the vulnerable-heart center of ourselves.

"Two are better than one because they have a good return for their labor. For if either of them falls, the one will lift up his companion" the Teacher in Ecclesiastes said.[2] We've experienced this push and pull in our lives, especially recently. When one of us is stressed and overwhelmed, anxious about the future, the other tends to be steady, calm, able to navigate the storm. There is great power to find shelter and stability in this neural intimacy.

I'd like to share another silly anecdote that could provide insight into this small, daily joy of our lives together . . .

. . . but you probably wouldn't get it. It's an inside joke.

---

1. Donne, "No Man Is an Island," All Poetry.
2. Eccl 4:9.

The Violence of the Given World

THE woods are loud with robin, cardinal, woodpecker, squirrel, and my two boys intent on making a more natural habitat for the toads they caught this morning. They stomp about and call out orders in their best impression of my father—an excavator and farmer—voices deep, authoritative, and abrupt. The toads are as tolerant as amphibians can be, scooped into damp hands and dropped in the driver's seat of a Tonka truck. Big Toad is the trucker today. Little Toad the train engineer.

Our deck positions me straight between the Toad Circus and the woods, lush with new May leaves that have formed a bright green canopy within the last two weeks. Oak, walnut, and dogwood are most prominent, with maple, spruce, and pine for variation here and there. Our land slopes fast to a grassy knoll, soggy all spring from snowmelt and rain, then descends to an engineered creek bed lined with railroad ties. The creek spills out abruptly where the railroad ties end to form a more natural waterfall, carving a way out through shale. My boys explore these woods and waterways, ever on the hunt for creepy crawlers they capture and contain in buckets.

We are suspended above the land, in the trees, eye level with what normally hides twenty feet above the groundcover. Everything is overgrown. Two weeks ago I carried loppers and pruners around the yard to prune and lop whatever ought not be there. Walnut saplings—gone. Rose of Sharon seedlings—gone. Low hanging limbs of flowering trees I cannot name—gone. In my frenzy I missed the poison ivy. Its rash spread everywhere on me, the only living species allergic to its oils while deer and bird dine contentedly on its seeds and waxy leaves (but clearly aren't hungry enough—you missed a patch, I want to say). Two weeks removed from

The Violence of the Given World

first exposure, I scratch and itch casually now. I warn my boys to avoid the wilting vines by the drive.

I am both amused and horrified by the toad show happening in my driveway—the way my boys take liberties with nature as if it is theirs to claim and master, as if they have been given dominion over the dirt of the earth and the rocks and these breathing creatures who just this morning were content to hide under groundcover. Now they take joy rides and race down our asphalt driveway with nothing but metal and plastic keeping them from being roadkill.

Six squirrels are arguing in the walnut tree. They are chasing each other's tails and running down the trunk and limbs as if there aren't dozens of feet between them and the forest floor. I see the leaves move first before the flurry of fur, hear the chitter before the race. My boys are bickering now, too, about their own ground and possessions, their rights, their justices, who should get the Tonka dump truck and who the car.

Toad's lungs fill and deflate, fill and deflate. He calls out a *10-4 good buddy* and pulls away. Does he know how soft his body is, how tenuous this ride? Does his body fill with air and adrenaline every time my son scoops him up from the dirt? They have squashed toads before, my sons. They are brutal, tender boys who do not know their power until it has been exerted, and then they grieve this final violence.

But first they hold their cupped hands up to me, *Mom, see, see*? Toad blinks and blinks.

※

Once, when I was young, I sat in the cab of the excavator with my father in the changing light of a summer evening, at the base of a sloping hill on my grandparents' farm. He was digging something, leveling something, evening out something, I don't know, and as the long arm of the boom reached up and out, and as the bucket split open the earth and lifted the dirt with its big metal fingers, a groundhog ran from some disturbed hiding place. Dad maneuvered the bucket with his levers to chase the varmint, and we laughed at its scurrying. It didn't run away, just around, darting in and out of the weeds and piles of dirt as we chased it with the bucket until it made one unexpected move into the path of our machine.

I had no malice in me, just delight to see the foreign creature run and play with us as if it had chosen this moment, heard the machine rumbling above its home the way my children hear the neighbor kids in their yard and dart out the door with a clash, forgetting their shoes in the frenzy to be among friends. But the groundhog didn't ask for this.

The tracks of the excavator lurched forward. The bucket swung on its hinge. The earth opened. "Where did the groundhog go?" I asked. "Back in his home," the answer. I learned later of my dad's attempts to hide death, how he dug a place for the small body and buried it without my noticing its lifelessness. I was a child captivated by all the world had to offer and offer up to her, willing and unwilling.

My boys want to know what to feed their wild toads. I am reluctant to look up such information. "I think they'd rather be free to hunt their own food, don't you?" I argue. There is such information in the world, however; it doesn't take much to find it. *Reptiles Magazine* offers an article on "American Toad Care and Husbandry," with advice to feed your wild toad three to six food items every other day, ranging from moth to grub to spider to slug and any other type of insect it can track and catch. With this new knowledge, I'm even more inclined to keep the toads free—go, eat, we have plenty of these insects and want fewer.

The chirping world must spy my sons and the captive toad. Surely they wait for stillness to circle in on the aluminum bucket habitat of mud and rock and lawn. The robin, the cardinal, the squirrel, the hawk, they chirp and chirp, a chaos of song and radio frequency, *10-4 good buddy*, song of joy and fear and hunger. Are they interested in such captive delicacies, such easy prey?

Just now, a solitary ant skittered across the deck. I bet he's on his way to tell his friends about something terrific, some morsel he's discovered they should all retrieve. My boys call down to the neighbor boy, skipping and leaping across the driveway, "Joel! Joel! We found *six* toads!" There are even more now, tender bodies hopping against the aluminum natural habitat. It will begin to feel like a plague, soon, the mass of them.

All this is happening. It just keeps happening, out of my control, within my control, beyond my control. I want to know what the bird in the tree above me is clacking about so incessantly—is it love, is it insects, is it just that it is and is happy to be? Everything is so busy being. Everything is so busy in its individual song, and then interruption. Foot in anthill. Hand under toad. Bucket through groundhog tunnel. Wind gust against nest. Loppers through new shoots of green. Squirrel against squirrel against squirrel against squirrel fighting for nuts and dominance and love.

※

It is the weekend after a school shooting. A boy used a revolver and a shotgun to kill a girl for rejecting him, and then he killed nine others and injured ten more for existing in a world in which someone could reject him. It's exhausting, this constant violence. I feel guilty for being so tired of summoning grief over *another school shooting*. We say these words now, "another school shooting," the way people in our region might say "another rainy day." It rained yesterday. It will rain tonight. It will rain on average 155 days here this year. What is the forecast? Another school shooting.

※

Violence is old, older than guns, older than cannons, older than swords, the same age as fists, as muscle, as stone. When Cain felt rejected by God, he murdered his brother in anger. *If I cannot have the blessing of Your love*, he said with his fists, *I will have the curse of his death. I would rather feel this pain than that emptiness.*

As a daughter of Eve, I cannot conceive of the violence of men, and yet they are the fruit of my womb. Fist of my fist. Bone of my bone. When I hold the toad my son hands me with delight in his eyes, it is with the same awe I felt when his own small body was first handed to me. He was intubated at birth, subdued so he would not pull the tubes from his own fragile lungs that forced his rib cage up and down in the ragged measurable breaths of not working quite right yet. This one is aware of the tenuous world. This one knows he is a miracle, and yet he is more inclined than his brother to test the precipice for danger. He is the one whose curiosity can turn malevolent, wonder turned to *I wonder what would happen if* . . . and then the end.

The toad's lungs fill and deflate.

※

Early childhood trauma shapes the brain's development such that a person may actually physiologically process the world differently. To my intubated-at-birth son, every discipline is a threat, every correction an accusation of unworthiness, every slight an opportunity to fight or retreat.

His fight-or-flight trigger has no safety mechanism. When he is angry or guilty or sad, all of him seems to crawl into himself.

I know he breathes because his chest rises and heaves. I know he is swirling in a mental frenzy because he clenches his fists, picks at his skin. I know he feels as if he is worthless because he destroys his room, destroys art he's created, destroys letters I've made for him declaring my love for him. I want so badly to reach him and help him when he lands here, but he vacates his eyes. He has no access to words. A therapist tells us to help him make sensory connections, to break the adrenaline driven sympathetic nervous system's hold, and this trick is like a miracle. *Tell me one thing you see. Tell me one thing you hear. Tell me one thing you smell. Eew, did you do that?* He laughs and there he is again, my son, my son.

There are six toads hopping in the aluminum bucket habitat. There is now a woodpecker in the tree beating holes to find food to kill to eat to consume to live to fly to be beautiful and violent and silent and loud and alive. There is wet earth, decomposing leaves, new saplings from fallen walnuts. Everything is happening, living and dying, risking and riding, *10-4 good buddy!*

The boys are giggling maniacally out of my line of sight. Their laughter is the kind that makes me worry for the toads. When I stand to look around the corner, my youngest son is holding a toad high above the bucket and looking to his brother, eager for approval.

"Don't—" I begin, but the toad is free now from his grasp, leaping, willing or unwilling, from three feet above the earth.

"You can't do that!" I yell, startling them both. "You'll hurt him dropping him from that high!"

The boys look surprised at this news. You mean they can't leap from three feet up and be okay? I don't know if they can leap from three feet up and be okay, but the maniacal laughter makes me think it doesn't matter.

I want my boys to grow up to be strong, tender men. Gentle strong men. Careful strong men. I want my boys to grow up to hold their children in their massive paws of hands and know the power in them to be strong violent but choose to be strong gentle, the way my husband holds them, the way my father held me. When they hurt someone or something, I want them to grieve.

The Violence of the Given World

The seventeen-year-old boy in Santa Fe "admitted he didn't shoot people he liked and meant to kill the ones he did target," but at least he has "cooperated with police," said "Yes, sir" when asked by the judge whether he wanted a court-appointed attorney.[1] He is a polite mass murderer. A considerate killer. A classmate said he was always really quiet.

What silences preceded the decision to load weapons onto the body and walk, or ride, or drive and hide? What filled the rattle of Cain's mind in those still moments, when morning breakfast bowls were still being eaten, steeling himself to cold, hard retaliation? What silences filled the shut doors of his room, what silences were pregnant with noise, the chaos so loud no one could stand to hear it and chose instead to ignore it?

Did Eve know Cain had the capacity to do what he did? Did she know of the rage, the jealousy, the way it could be uncapped; did she try to tame the fury early, coaxing every temper down to clenched fists, relaxed, deep breaths. *Tell me one thing you see. Tell me one thing you hear. Tell me one thing you smell.* Did she teach him his manners, tell him to say, "Yes, sir. No, sir. Sorry, ma'am"? I'm going to use this body you gave me as a weapon, ma'am. I'm going to use your guns to kill people, sir. I'm going to see the fragile world around me and dominate it, sir, crush it, impose my power on it, sir.

What mother, hand pressed to pregnant belly, could ever dream of that one promised son and fathom the coming fracture of her love, her grief, her fury?

※

Eve isn't given many words, just another son, one to replace Abel, and that son has a son. The lineage of Cain is one of vengeance: sons who reference their father's curse and curse exponentially those who threaten them. Somehow, Eve crawls out of her grief and makes love again to Adam, son of God made from dust and breath, to conceive again a child who will turn from her to use his strength, violent or gentle. Somehow, she loves and loves again, love throbbing broken and healed, broken and healed, broken and healed.

※

1. Hanna, et al., "Alleged shooter at Texas high school spared people he liked, court document says," *CNN*.

Ordinary Time

My sons are at it again. They are each holding a toad in their cupped hands. I watch, take in the birdsong and squirrel chatter and breathing and blinking toads, the violence of the given world, and wait for what will happen next.

Little Joys: The Woods

UNTIL we lived on a property with pine trees, I never appreciated the seasonality of evergreens. Our pines, rhododendrons, arborvitae, and spruce have growing seasons and seasons of dormancy, times when they are more aromatic and times when they drop their needles. We planted some trees in the last few years, and when I see their new height and bright, fresh growth, I feel proud, as if I had anything to do with it.

There was a moment in 2020 when our spruce trees started dropping their lower branches, so much so that it was alarming. Google said that trees will do that sometimes; if they have reason to believe it's going to be a hard winter, they'll reduce the things they carry to ensure their own survival. It was like the spruce trees were reading the universe for signs of global pandemic. I noticed it right around the time I was deciding to resign from my job to make space for recovery. Maybe we were sharing the same air, saying the same prayers. Maybe they had their own form of long COVID.

Around the same time, our pine trees produced an exorbitant number of pine cones. I mentioned this to our arborist (the lady we bought our new trees from), and she said she'd noticed the same thing, and it usually meant we should expect a lot of snow. The pine trees know their lives are short, even though most live between 100 and 200 years. They know they are mortal. They will ensure the legacy of their species, even if it's the last thing they do.

Since the beginning of the pandemic, I've taken every opportunity to take my work outdoors, onto our deck, where I can sit among the trees' canopies. I watch the squirrels, because my dogs tell me to, and listen to songbirds, hawks, and crows call to one another from the trees. All around me, there are stalwart trees, holding the soil on the hill, casting down their leaves, interrupting the wind. I take great comfort in their constancy. The squirrels hustle from tree to tree, the birds flit between branches, there one day, gone the next, the deer haunt the underbrush so quietly you're more likely to miss them than spy them.

But every day, the trees are there. It is a comfort to be surrounded by things that have existed before me, that are taller than me, stronger than me, and will last longer than me. The woods are models of perseverance and suffering. They drop what they can no longer carry. They are rooted in the earth and reaching toward the sky. They grow. They make room for others in their shade and shadows. Even in their dying, they accommodate the living, becoming a sanctuary for insects and fungi, squirrels, foxes, deer, coyotes, and mice.

In the morning when I rise, I look out our bedroom window to see if all these witnesses still keep watch, to see how we will together greet the day.

Advent and Everything After

"Elvis, did you do your homework?"

The question sets off the grand finale fireworks show in my son's head. "AUGHHHH!" he moans, every bone in his body suddenly rubber. He is a heap of laundry on the floor, a flailing pile of skin and bones, a tortured, possessed twelve-year-old with the incredible burden of *homework* and *turning stuff in*. See also, *taking out the trash* and *showering*.

The preteen battle would be tolerable and expected if it wasn't for the recent turn in outbursts. "I CAN'T!" and "I'M THE WORST SON EVER!" erupt from his lips as if it takes too much energy to keep holding in this internal chaos any longer. Papers, sheets, blankets, stuffed animals, and clothes are tossed and crumpled around his room.

I try rational conversation. "Why do you feel this way?"

Elvis rings his hands, clenches his fists, works his jaw muscles. No one can reach him when he's like this, and if I keep trying and pushing, we only meet each other in escalation. There've been nights in the past when we've gone at it for hours, getting in wrestling matches, pinning each other to the bed, shouting in each other's faces, me just about out of my right mind before leaping back to my senses and leaving the room, exhausted and resigned.

When he finally comes down, he's apologetic and aims to repair relationships; we accept apologies and extend forgiveness, but nothing is different. Tomorrow night will be the same tiptoe toward trying to help him shift gears, empty the dishwasher, turn in a homework assignment, or turn off the TV, any one request the potential trigger to set off an internal detonation of self-loathing and anger we are ultimately helpless to solve.

There has to be more to it than hormones.

Elvis started evacuating his body in moments of discipline or direction sometime in elementary school. He couldn't shift gears, and asking him to turn off a video game or put on his shoes—or any other number of activities that drew him away from whatever he was currently doing—resulted in a body-flailing tantrum or long blank stares into the distance while we kept rambling on, trying to get him to engage. It was as if any conflict rendered him mute, incapable of articulating his thoughts or emotions.

The behavior felt like disobedience, disregard for our authority. *He's so stubborn*, we said.

My best friend was pursuing her master's degree in counseling at the time, and she asked me to proofread her paper on early childhood trauma and its physiological effects on brain development. The editor in me was delighted. I love to find things to fix, to make things right. She wrote about how even a traumatic birth experience could cause a child's brain to develop in such a way as to constantly be in fight-or-flight mode, ever on the edge to try to protect itself from an obviously dangerous world.

Her paper made my skin prickle. Could this describe Elvis, my son who spent ten days in the NICU immediately after birth, who left the safety of the womb and entered a world that threatened to kill him for lack of oxygen? Coming out of the NICU, the doctors assured us he'd have a full physical recovery, no symptoms or breathing issues after his initial inability to breathe on his own. After all of those machines, all of that monitoring, they let us just take him home. No one said our son who survived a near-death birth experience might develop PTSD.

The self-disgust started earlier this fall with middle school. Despite his perfectionism, Elvis started failing classes simply because he wasn't turning anything in. He's super smart and capable, never struggled to turn in assignments in the past. I couldn't understand it. When we tried to coach him through and encourage him to do the work, he despaired that he wasn't capable of learning responsibility. He was adamant. He could not do it. *I am worthless. I am defective. I am the worst son. I don't deserve to live.*

I remembered my own low self-esteem, my own inability to articulate my emotions, my own scrambled thoughts and failure to get out of my own head. I built arguments and counterarguments for what would happen if I said how I actually felt. I rationalized away my sadness or anger with theories of how people would respond if I spoke up, and playing out all of those scenarios would keep whatever emotional storm I was weathering locked inside my brain.

In short, I felt terrible for Elvis in moments like this. There's nothing worse than wanting so badly for someone to know how you feel but when pressed to speak, to feel absolutely at a loss for how to say what you need to say. There's too much noise to find the clarity to speak. My husband, the utmost external processor, doesn't understand this. When Elvis retreats into his inner world, Brandon tends to press in, and Elvis retreats more, so Brandon presses in further, louder, and the noise inside amplifies until the spirit in Elvis's eyes disappears. He is standing there and words are being said to him but he isn't listening anymore. He has left his body in the room to go somewhere safe, somewhere the storm can't disturb.

I can't bear these moments. It's been one of the ongoing points of contention in our marriage—how to parent our unresponsive middle son in moments of utter stubbornness. The more Brandon presses in, the more I back off, retreat into my own corner and wait for the noise to die down. Brandon is flabbergasted and frustrated with my lack of engagement. *You're letting him get away with so much.* I'm flabbergasted and frustrated that he can't see how ineffective this approach to handling Elvis is. *He's not even there right now, can't you see?* I don't have any answers either. We're both at a loss for what to do. Elvis is gone, in his room, destroying works of art and tearing the sheets from his bed.

I wait. I wait and wait. I find my husband first. And then I find my son.

※

During our intake appointment at Cornerstone Counseling, the counselor, Sharon, asks me why I've brought Elvis in for counseling, and I explain the latest behaviors. Elvis is sitting right there, listening, and I feel like I'm ratting him out, but all I really want is for Elvis to know how much I love him and for him to have it a little easier. Middle school is hard, and life is going to get harder. He's a great kid, so smart, so capable, but he has started to say things that worry me. They worry me right now, in the minor struggles of middle school, and they worry me for the future. If these things can trigger self-loathing, what about bigger failures? Larger disappointments? If he can't learn how to cope now, will he be able to cope later? The unspoken fears for future Elvis lodge in my throat.

Sharon asks about the traumatic moments I mentioned on the intake form. I share briefly about his birth, the near drowning incident when he was four, kidney stones when he was five.

Elvis chimes in, "And I fell off the front of my bike that year, too, knocking out my front teeth."

I hadn't remembered how closely all of these things had happened for him. In all of the daily monotony of parenting young people and personal crises, it wasn't evident to me what a traumatic year four to five must have been for him. Listing off this series of events so matter-of-factly makes me wonder at resilience, how I'm even here in this office, still married, still parenting this fragile strong child. I'm struck again by the mercies of scientific miracles and miraculous science that have kept all of us alive and together this long; how fortunate, how blessed, how randomly wonderful it is to be a human in this age.

Sharon is in her seventies, I think, and she is a slow talker, a long pauser. It's almost too warm in her office, and every time we're there I have to keep nudging Elvis to keep him awake. It makes me want to fold into the cushions as well and just rest a while. Maybe that's the point.

Sharon happens to be licensed to provide Eye Movement Desensitization and Reprocessing, or EMDR, therapy. She explains that she would have retired a decade ago but she's found this therapy so effective and the results so fun that she doesn't want to give it up, so she just keeps practicing.

EMDR therapy is used to treat individuals who struggle with traumatic memories. It turns out that the body remembers trauma—even trauma the cognitive mind can't remember. Using this device that vibrates in various rhythms with paddles that remind me of a video-game controller, Sharon explains how she plans to help Elvis reprocess these traumatic memories. She draws a picture of a brain to help explain the places where memories are stored before cognitive memories are formed. The limbic system is working hard to keep Elvis safe, even when he isn't in any physical danger, which triggers heightened fight-or-flight responses, increases adrenaline, and creates a constant hum of anxiety Elvis probably doesn't even notice because it's been with him since right after birth. To help Elvis reprocess his birth memory, which he obviously doesn't remember, Sharon asks me to write his birth story. I'm a little skeptical but mostly excited and eager to get started. Elvis appears hopeful—reassured, perhaps.

The third counseling appointment for Elvis is scheduled for late November, right before Advent. Sharon had forgotten our plan to reprocess Elvis's birth memory at our second appointment, and so I've been waiting, a folded two-page, direct-address version of Elvis's birth story tucked inside my purse until the counseling appointment. I can hardly wait.

Advent is our family's favorite season, a season of intentionality. For the last decade we've planned daily Advent activities leading up to Christmas, sometimes with heavier spiritual overtones and sometimes just with lots of winter fun. In the Christian liturgical calendar, Advent is the long wait before an awakening, the season of longing for what we don't yet know, hope for what we cannot yet see. As American Protestant Christians we tend to celebrate Advent like it's already Christmas, like the hope has already arrived, like God has already shown His true Self to us. It's hard to pause, to stay in the mindset of waiting and longing, when the whole culture is in a frenzied state of manufactured celebration.

At this counseling appointment, we stand on the edge of Advent, and from this ledge I hope for what I cannot yet see.

For how often we've referenced Elvis's birth story—passing by Akron Children's Hospital, noting how he almost died, remembering the miracles—it occurs to me prior to our appointment that he doesn't know all of the details. He hasn't heard from start to finish how it went. As Elvis holds the EMDR paddles set to a low and slow rhythm in order to access the pre-memory memories stored somewhere in his body, I unfold my paper and begin to read:

> We knew the exact hour of your birth because it was a scheduled C-section, so we went to the hospital ready and excited to meet you. Dad and I had been talking about naming you Elvis for months, but I still wasn't convinced it was the name for you. We waited in the surgery prep room to go back. As we waited, a really long infomercial for Elvis Presley came on, and Dad said, "It's a sign!" I rolled my eyes and said that if you came out with dark hair and sideburns we would name you Elvis.
>
> They wheeled me back to the surgery area, and everything looked like it was going to be just fine—the nurses and doctors joked about how Elvis was getting ready to leave the building (of my body, that is). But when you were born, one nurse noticed that something wasn't quite right about how you were crying. It

just didn't sound like a normal newborn cry to her. Everyone else said that you sounded like a real squaller, and for a minute people laughed because of how Elvis is such a great singer and all, but that one nurse knew you were struggling. She quickly took action while the doctors finished with me.

They took you to the neonatal intensive care unit, called NICU, because you were struggling to breathe and you were also having pulmonary hypertension, which is like baby heart attacks. I didn't get to see you right after you were born. It was a couple hours before I could see you—I had to recover from surgery and they were working hard to stabilize you.

While I was in recovery, Dad showed me a photo of you, and we laughed that you actually HAD dark hair and sideburns, so we decided to name you Elvis—it was meant to be. Dad told me how sick you were, but I didn't believe how sick you were until they wheeled me to the nursery, where they were preparing you to go to another hospital—Akron Children's Hospital. You were lying in this plastic case with all kinds of wires and tubes and machines connected to you. They had given you medicine to put you to sleep because you kept trying to pull the tubes out—you were such a fighter, even on the first day of your life!

I couldn't touch you yet because your heart and lungs were working so hard to try to keep working right. They took you by ambulance to Akron Children's Hospital, which wasn't very far to go, but it felt super far to me. You went by yourself with the nurses and doctors. Even though I'd just had surgery, they let me leave the hospital early so I could be with you.

When we got to the hospital, there were twenty other babies in the NICU. The babies were put in order of most serious to least, and you were in bed #1. Your diagnosis was pulmonary hypertension and respiratory distress syndrome, which meant that your lungs hadn't developed everything they needed in order to work right at first. Everyone we knew was praying for you. After the first couple days of being in the hospital, the doctors said they couldn't figure it out but it looked like you didn't have pulmonary hypertension after all. We knew that it was a miracle at work.

Dad and I spent every possible minute we could with you at the hospital. Grandma Rose and Pop-Pop, Granny and Pop, Lydia, and your uncles all came to visit you. You were so sick that for the first few days we weren't allowed to touch you, we could only look through the plastic. The nurses gave me a little bear that they said I should hold and rub against my skin so that we could put the bear in with you. I think that's why you love stuffed animals so much.

You were so tough and stubborn, you just kept hanging in there. When I finally got to hold you, the nurses let me put my hands underneath your little body, which was still on medicine to keep you from moving, while they changed your diaper and adjusted your wires.

Those days were so long and scary, but when I was driving back and forth from the hospital, I felt this overwhelming peace from God that everything was going to be okay. It gave me strength and faith and hope that you would be healed. The first week in the hospital seemed to go on forever. Everyone just loved our little Elvis—the nurses all said what a tough little boy we had. The doctors encouraged us with updates on your progress, which was slow at first, and then suddenly everything started to get better. Soon we could hold your hand and you grabbed ahold of our finger and wouldn't let go! Then you started breathing on your own and they took the tubes out. Soon you were opening your eyes and ready for us to take you out of the crib. I remember how grateful I was to be able to put you against my chest and kiss the top of your head. You made it! You had survived!

After the first week in the NICU, you got better really fast. Once you could leave the incubator, you started to eat without the feeding tube; it was time to go home. The nurses and doctors were so excited to wish you well and to be able to say, officially, that Elvis was ready to leave the building. I was always so amazed at how fragile you were in those early days but at the same time how strong and resilient, how powerful and able to overcome such a difficult task. It showed me that you would be able to conquer anything later in life. Dad and I were so relieved and excited to bring you home, safe and healthy.

I refold the paper and take a deep breath. Sharon asks Elvis how hearing this story makes him feel on a scale of 1–10, and he places the discomfort around a six. She asks him where the discomfort is in his body, and he says his stomach. I remember his colicky first weeks, when antibiotics wiped out both good and bad bacteria until we remedied with probiotics so he could eat in comfort. She tells him to close his eyes and hold the paddles again. She runs the EMDR therapy through three or four times, and each time the memory's discomfort drops on the scale and moves, first to his chest (no surfactant, no air), then to his right cheek (the feeding tube taped against his face), then to his forehead (the scalp IV, the monitors, the beeping, the machines).

I am silenced. I am in wonder.

Sharon says that it might take a couple of days to notice any difference, and maybe he will notice no difference at all, but if he does, he might feel lighter and be able to think clearer. She describes the sensation as if the world is suddenly running at a slower pace. We leave the office after scheduling a follow-up appointment for after Christmas.

Elvis isn't one to volunteer information typically, so I ask him what he thought about hearing his birth story. "I feel . . . kind of wonderful. I didn't realize that all that time I was in the hospital, I was never alone. Someone was always with me."

※

When Isaiah prophesied the coming Messiah, he said that He would be called Immanuel, which means God with us. It is the promise of the long waiting of Advent fulfilled, Christ with us, God with us, Love with us. My children know that Christmas is coming. Even though we hold out our hope and try not to celebrate early, we celebrate anyway because the revelation is here already for us, true already for us, Christ is with us, Love is with us, has been with us, will be with us. If Advent is our season of anticipation, Christmas is the resounding celebration that what we were waiting for all that time was here with us all along.

We just had to reprocess the memory.

※

During the weeks that follow the birth story appointment, Elvis is different. He makes jokes at dinner. When prompted about homework and catching up on stuff, he says, "I'm working on it." And he is. While I drive us around to look at Christmas lights, he offers his latest theological consideration of Genesis and the Creation account and scientific advancements. He wonders out loud about things. I ask him to take out the trash, and he *does*. It isn't that he's changed, per se, he's just more fully himself, the Elvis I've gotten to see in bits and moments but never this at ease, never this relaxed. There's less noise in the way.

Days pass. There are no tantrums. I make meaningful eye contact with my husband and grin foolish, happy grins. I want to sing, I want to shout, everything in me threatens to spill over in joy any second of every day, my son, my son, he has returned to me at last, at last.

Of course, he's still a twelve-year-old boy who has opinions and wishes that differ from his parents, but they don't trigger volcanic eruptions. He still wants to play video games longer than we'd like. He still would rather not do chores. But he has words, and I can hear him, I can see him, yes, there he is. There he is.

※

So much time is spent in the long waiting between Advents, Lents, and Epiphanies. The waiting is accompanied by a low hum, a background static I don't think I even notice until the buzz finally breaks. When the whirling wind on the mountain dies down, when the wrestling angel gives up its hold, when the labor ends and the child cries in the silent night, peace isn't just the absence of anxiety but also the presence of something else, something more. What was before is supplanted by goodness and grace. There is no going back to the way things were before, there's only memory reprocessed, the cyclical turn of the calendar to remind us of where we have been and how we might have hope for the things to come in these ordinary and extraordinary times.

※

"Elvis," I ask weeks into the Advent season, "have you noticed a difference since our counseling appointment?"

He smiles. "Maybe," he says, "do you want me to go back to the way I was before?"

I laugh. "I loved you before, but I also really like how things are now."

Sabbath Afternoon

If you haven't done so lately, it's time to grab a picnic blanket before the warm days slip away and the evening sun skitters over the horizon in the hurry of new autumn notebooks and backpacks; before it gets too dark too early for leisure and stillness, grab the hem of a handmade quilt and lift it up until the air carries it like a flying carpet down softly to the ground, under a tall oak tree where the grass is cool but not damp yet from falling dew, and kneel, then fold over in child's pose if you do yoga or just bow for a minute prostrate and breathe in the scent of your laundry detergent or dryer sheet mingled with the earthy earthiness of the dirt, then breathe out through your mouth and feel the carbon dioxide and oxygen press against your nose and cheeks and forehead which is also pressed against the cloth, which is pressed against the cool top shelf of the Earth, all topsoil and mulch and decomposing plant matter that you will be one day, just plant matter some worm will worm its way through on its way to making a new body out of what is no longer filled with spirit; but fear not because you are here, after all, paused on this nearly autumn day and the wind is moving like the Spirit, rustling the leaves like the Spirit, sending goosebumps up and down your arms like the Spirit, and it is quiet, more quiet than you've been in days or weeks, maybe even months, maybe even years—how long has it been since you've paused like this on a blanket in the shade of a tall oak tree?—did you just hear a bird, or was that a cricket or a frog's mating trill; what time is it? It isn't time yet to get up but stretch out now on your belly, and use the word "belly" because it's such a round and jolly word and reminds you of Santa and his bowl full of jelly, and your belly is happy flattened against the cool of the earth and the smooth cloth of your quilt; maybe now is the time to turn your head for just one second, or two or three or four, and stare into the wild jungle that is this lawn of monocot blades and superheroes—have you seen them?—these ants, they can carry up to 5,000 times their weight before losing their heads; there one goes right now with a crumb of leaf in its jaws, so be still. You may feel like you are carrying a heavy burden, but do not be afraid; you are worth many heads of ants and you are here, you are here, you are here, welcome to the world, this world so full of many bright things, even slugs and potato bugs you can see scurrying or slurping—isn't that what slugs are doing?—moving, anyway, through the cool of the earth, and from this angle everything seems much smaller, more bearable, all in rhythm, even your heartbeat that you can feel in tandem motion with the movement of the earth's own drumbeat. Don't you know that even this was ordained, this was incarnated back when God created the heavens and the earth, the earth, it is good, and you, you are very good, so now rest. Be still and know that He is God and good and here, in the threads of this blanket, in the threads of the grass, in the threads of your DNA, and He is gentle and humble in heart, and His yoke is easy, and His burden is light, much lighter than 5,000 times your weight, so do not lose your head. Rest, if you haven't lately. Here's your invitation to Sabbath a second some Saturday or weekday afternoon while the world keeps turning, so you can observe it and all that God has placed here as a reminder: yes, there it goes again, the ant so busy with such a heavy load and yet it is carried, by grace, it is carried. Breathe again and let the world in to be loved because He first loved us and it, and who cares if the grass needs mowed, this moment is only a little while in all of eternity and eternity is held within it—the dirt, the worm, the wind, and you, so be still if you haven't lately.

Little Joys: Books

This year, I've traveled through the desert on horseback with a shepherd and an alchemist. I've fished the lakes of Canada by canoe, attended a boy's boarding school, learned the dance of the herons along a river, sat in the kitchen of a distressed and impoverished wife in Michigan, explored vocation, followed a friend as she sought out her origin story, listened to veterans returning from foreign wars, walked from refugee camp to refugee camp with my older sister in Rwanda, played with magical creatures within view of a cerulean sea, smuggled my Jewish friend to safety, searched the globe for a safe place for a transgendered child, sat in isolation after sordid affairs, sought the Virgin Mary statue of my youth, magnified Ohio's natural landscape, surveyed a century of macroeconomics, hurried across the Mexican border with a heroin dealer and observed a doctor prescribe painkillers along the Ohio River, and delighted in the minutiae that makes life marvelous.

Every book is an expedition into a meticulously crafted, imagined world that was born in the mind of a writer. Books are a glimpse into other people's souls, a portal into other people's minds. Not only do I experience far more than my own life is able to accomplish, I get to do so with at least one other companion, the author who journeyed to that foreign land first. What surprises, what delights, what challenges they encountered as they set out to create something that did not exist before!

Then, after many rejections and negotiations, drafts and delays, that author sent their final manuscript to print, and an editor reviewed it, and a publisher forwarded it to the printing press, and a press operator programmed the press, and the pages came, and the ink dried. The paper was folded and cut and glued and bound and boxed and shipped, and now, finally, anyone can enter into one author's story. Anyone can enter into one author's mind.

Above me while I write are probably 400 different books, 400 different tales, 400 different angles and perspectives, 400 different journeys that took years to live and years more to write before they became these bound volumes honoring fragments of life that come together to form a mosaic of humanity. Over 3 million more are published annually, added to the stack of human testament to creativity, ingenuity, imagination, and faith that there are yet more stories to tell, yet more life to live, yet more depths of the human experience to explore.

Foxglove, Bee Balm

Bee balm. Foxglove.

These words have been missing for me for days and here they are, suddenly, arriving as I listen to Bill Bryson read his book, *At Home*, driving the length of highway that connects my current home in Copley Township with my urban office. It is the chapter on the history of gardens. Perhaps these words arrive at this moment because I have spent so much time coming and going from the gardens I have loved: leaving the gardens of my youth in Geauga County each summer where I walked the acres and acres of tall cornstalks and long plots of tomato vines to return to the industrial rooms of middle school; leaving the landscape beds at Six Flags I tended two summers to go back to college; leaving the flowers my mom and I split and rearranged around our home to grow my own roses and plant a brick patio behind the first house I owned with my husband, then going again to the garden we tilled and cultivated and planted with our three children on our postage-stamp property in Ashland; only to leave again, now, to this garden.

I have inherited, for the time being, my husband's grandmother Garnet's gardens and tend the beds she planned and planted. Her grandchildren and great-grandchildren scamper and dash and dig on this property in Copley. Garnet and her husband Delbert bought this lot and built this house fifty-four years ago, when my husband's dad was eleven, just two years older than my daughter is now.

I never expected to move here or to want to settle here. There's no doubt that I'm a sucker for all things nostalgic, even those that aren't directly tied to me, but when my husband first suggested the idea—a solution to the next coming and going of changing jobs and communities, without carrying two mortgages—I crinkled my nose at it.

"But it's *Grandma's* house," I whined.

It smelled like Grandma's house. Even though my in-laws had made significant progress emptying out the accumulations of twist ties and plastic bags, funeral notices and old greeting cards, magazines from the 1970s and empty gallon jugs, there was still so much *stuff*, musty and dusty, mothballs and mold and so many reminders of her. Her furniture was arranged exactly as it had been since she'd moved out two years earlier, when she was unable to stay any longer, unable to figure out why it was so hot in her house, why the pot had burnt down black, how to operate the microwave.

"Maybe just for a time, only for a season," I reasoned, prepared to make some other foreign house nearer to my new job our home. In the meantime, we'd use this place as our transition. A layover between one plot and another.

Now it is spring. We have inhabited this space for six months, slowly going from "let's go back to the house—Grandma's house" to "let's head home." It is *our* furniture that mingles now with hers in the living room, our pots and cookie trays in *our* cabinets, the same floral carpeting and good-bad draperies left in place until a later date, hanging in *our* bedrooms.

But it's the outside that carries her strongest memory, her greatest presence. Bleeding hearts are popping up everywhere this spring in the spaces we cleared away upon moving in last fall. There had been all this overgrowth and weeds, trees rotting outward from their heartwood, ground that settled toward the foundation so that rainwater rolled down the side of the basement and inward. Mold. Moss. Rot. Weeds. But the ground now around the house slants away, and we have shaped new landscape beds.

Seeds of plants forgotten bloom; their flowers are pale hearts wilting to seeds. I marvel at it all, new buds and new shoots, plants I don't initially recognize, some that look like weeds at first, only to flower.

Garnet isn't gone from this earth yet, but she's gone, into assisted living and hiding her illness well: grandmother fading slowly. It comes and goes. Before she stopped recognizing us, she visited and remarked what a nice place we have. So many flowerbeds! Now when we visit her, it's unclear to me whether she knows who I am. I am sure she knows that my kids somehow belong to her. There is something at the cellular level that connects her fading synapses so that recognition lights her eyes when my husband or father-in-law are near. The blood level of things binds the physical to the ethereal, the present to some far distant memory. *Yes, these are Brandon's kids! My great-grandchildren! My seed, my fruit, my vine, these are mine.*

To me, she is polite and kind. We are strangers.

❦

I wanted to call the foxglove "wolfsbane."

When the perennial beds began to grow this spring there were leaves of plants I couldn't name, green fan-shaped fronds, soft rabbit's ear-like leaves, and a tall, wispy stalk that I thought might be garden phlox. The plant with the fan-shaped leaves was sprouting in all kinds of places around the yard, and since it didn't look familiar, I figured it wasn't just another weed, but what? What could it be? When the full cone of flower buds pushed up, I knew I wanted to keep it.

Something in me knew the plant name I was looking for had an animal in it.

❦

These words—foxglove, bee balm—words I have known, like song titles or actors' names, are always just out of reach. I imagine a gap between question and answer stretching across the great divide of left and right brain, neurons of language reaching, reaching into nothingness but knowing there's something; surely I know this. What is it? Not wolfsbane. The names come and go; I can picture that one actress, you know the one, my mother's doppelganger, dark hair, wide smile, *Miss Congeniality*? How many times I have gestured with my hands in a circle, willing the words to my lips as if they were buried in my gut and just need to be heaved out.

And then, like a bridge, Bill Bryson reads his history of British landscaping and just like that, the words come gliding out, diving off the tip of my tongue. "Foxglove! Bee balm!" I chant in the car, elated to have found them, my lost vocabulary.

❦

"I was going to get the ... you know ... ." Garnet explains in the middle of the night, awake again for the third time, visiting the kitchen at my in-laws' house. This is before we move to her house, before her dementia advances beyond the point of home care. "I need a cup of water," she tells me, holding in her hand another cup, another one to line the windowsill in her room, abandoned, their purposes forgotten.

※

Before I found their names, I split the foxglove and bee balm and transplanted them around the house to the new flowerbeds, unsure of what would bloom and where. The bleeding hearts were a surprise. I hadn't seen them growing in her yard before we moved in, but now they've sprouted all over the place, in almost every flowerbed. The instant I find them I am transported to the limestone gravel sidewalk leading to a colonial blue house with colonial blue steps and a thick shrub of dark green foliage, sprays of hundreds of hearts in arches against the cool foundation, and my grandmother's blue pitcher filled with bright red fruit punch, and my flip-flops slapping on the wooden steps, the screen door swinging on its hinge and slamming shut, the dark interior of my grandma's house in summer with the shades drawn to keep the heat out, the heaviness of that pitcher of sugar water as I tried to pour some into a red Solo cup. My cousins would be out there, waiting for me to come back to play ball or TV tag. Or maybe we were taking turns on the rope swing under the tall maples that lined the lane, spinning each other dizzy till we felt we might lose our lunches on the lawn.

"Stop! Stop!" I shrieked, running in to get my drink.

But now it is a different grandmother's house and I am so much older. My sons are in the sandbox here, and then they are running with the neighbor kids. My daughter's basketball throbs against the cement her great-grandparents poured several decades ago, and I am finding more species of lilies to split and divide and plant next to bleeding hearts.

The bleeding heart's scientific name is *Lamprocapnos spectabilis*. It is a spectacle here, and I save each offshoot I discover, worried to disturb its roots too much. Originally from Asia and introduced to European gardens in the 1800s, it is not native to this place either, but what is anymore?

We turn over old landscape beds grown over with thick groundcover and a mess of variegated hostas so that my dad can backfill the foundation, to keep the rainwater from running toward the basement. I keep the blue star juniper and move the lacy ferns, tell my dad to just knock over the rotting dogwoods. The pruning we did each year to save the trees was in vain. It is so easy to clear away these decades of growth, and yet the bleeding hearts return, the bleeding hearts grow.

Ordinary Time

※

Bill Bryson spends his book *At Home* coming and going from his house in England, back through history to the beginnings of domestic life only to return again to his country parsonage, its cool stone walls, its nooks and crannies, its modifications and renovations. I wonder if he ever wanders room to room now, the past and present whirling around him. The people who came before him are only spirits, buried in tax records and graveyards or mentioned in old newspaper archives, maybe a sketch or a frowning photograph. They are only known by what little is left behind.

I did not know Garnet when she planned the arching trellis near the back of our half-acre, nor did I know how long the wisteria vine stretched up and over before it withered to a rotted stump. I did not know Garnet before her husband Delbert died, before my husband helped her design the front landscape beds with their boxwoods and ugly purpleleaf sand cherries I would have advised against had I been here. I did not know Garnet when she and Delbert decided to add a few more pin oaks to the back lawn, and if I had I would have said, no, these are too close together, and right in the middle of the perfect backyard baseball field—didn't you think about your future great-grandchildren when you chose to stretch that long garden bed that splits the lawn in half, and didn't you think about how tall the trees would reach, and how far the shadows would fall, and how quickly the yard can go from full sun to full shade, and how all that you thought was permanent is so very transient? Didn't you know this, didn't you see it coming, the way the words sometimes just disappear, the way you can know something all your life and then suddenly forget it?

It works in reverse as well, see, memory lying dormant for decades and then there it is, that red Kool-Aid in a blue pitcher, long summers, all triggered in a single bleeding heart.

My mom planted a wisteria vine once, next to the side of their new living room addition. It creeped and trailed itself, attaching its strands like sticky frog legs to cling to the siding and reach its way ever higher, over the gutter and up toward the roofline. I loved those subtle greens and purples, its grape cluster blooms so casual. It grew and grew and grew, so fast and aggressive against the house, its vines lifting the gutter away from the siding, squeezing the deck's wooden railing. You don't realize the pull of vegetation, its strength and resilience, how it can change the landscape or cause disturbance, even destroying foundations if planted too near the basement or too close to a sidewalk. Roots have the power to lift concrete.

Trees can wrap their trunks around barbed wire and hold it there long after the fence is gone. A rotted stump can look like it's been dead for decades until suddenly one afternoon, you are weeding along the perimeter of your husband's grandmother's property to see a single wisteria vine inching its way out again, remembering what it was like to be alive.

※

It is thought that dementia might be caused by a lifelong series of ministrokes. First you forget where you left your keys. A few decades later and you forget where you parked your car. A few decades later and you forget who you are. Gaps expand in the brain, a slow erasure until all is still, all is calm.

※

What is wolfsbane? That's what I wanted to call the foxglove in the garden. Wolf turned to fox. It's a plant named after an animal. These are the crossed paths and confused neurons at play in my brain, almost funny. Bane, though, is something that ruins or spoils, something poisonous. A glove protects.

My mother-in-law, Rhonda, is known for these associations. Shopping for her teenaged son, she told the sales rep she was looking for a CD by a band, "I think it's Wet Frog on a Bike in the Rain."

He said, "You mean, Toad the Wet Sprocket?"

"Whatever!" Rhonda likely laughed, loud and full, uninhibited and unconcerned about this frequent memory twitch.

But Garnet once told her, "You're not blood. You don't matter," and the memory of that is a live wire of synapses, never far from her. Wolfsbane. Poison. And yet Rhonda was able to swallow it. She made Garnet breakfast and coffee, unlaced her tennis shoes, persuaded her to bathe, led her back to bed, took out her hearing aids, helped her undress, and then waded with her through the twilight of dementia again, night after night, until she moved into the memory care unit. Sometimes Garnet seemed to forget her daughter-in-law was her daughter-in-law, and then she was kind. Polite. Grateful.

Foxglove. Protection.

※

Now the bee balm is blooming, and I know it has something to do with an insect when I stretch my fingers back in the recesses of the garden bed for some forgotten reference book of perennials. But just as quickly as foxglove came on my drive home, when I wasn't even looking for the name, there it is: bee balm, something that sounds like it should be soothing against a sting. Its scientific name is *monarda*. This too triggers some chemical electricity, and I immediately think *monarch*, then, *how can I find milkweed to plant in these flowerbeds?* Just as swiftly, I am hunting through the fields and finding caterpillars on milky leaves as a child on my way to young adulthood, chrysalis in the process of transformation, no longer caterpillar and not quite butterfly.

Garnet watches her great-grandchildren with unobstructed delight but possibly does not know they are hers. Possibly only knows for a second they are kin. *These are mine. I don't know how or who but yes.*

It looks like a coffin, this mummification against the milkweed. She is in the chrysalis, I think, her former self gradually fading, falling away. There are simple pleasures left, now: children, grandchildren, warmth, dessert, birds. Soon there will be no words. I don't know what happens next, what happens to the soul when body and mind slip into unconsciousness. Do we make return visits, are there round trips from one place of leaving to another, or does life before appear again in an instant, triggered by some distant object now near, the past and future layered transparencies of wisteria, blue pitchers, and bleeding hearts?

This slipping away, maybe it is yet another metamorphosis, the slit in the chrysalis indiscernible to the caterpillar but the next adventure to the monarch, drying out, taking flight, past life a memory faint as it lifts off to kiss the phlox, the foxglove, the bee balm.

Mothers' Top Dresser Drawers

To rummage there was to be let in on a secret. You whispered. You tiptoed. Among the satin, lace, and letters of my mother's was a string of pearls I let trickle across my palm. It had clung to the collarbone of her grandmother, my great-grandmother, Anna B., the one who claimed to be born on the boat coming from Slovakia. Mom and I would roll our eyes. We both would have died in childbirth, we believed, without modern medicine. Sure, born on the boat.

I have since worn such necklaces with proper office attire for important meetings where I told grown men what to do with their business's marketing budgets, and they listened. I felt brave. I even drove my own car there and back as if we women have always been doing such things. Anna B., that supposedly water-birthed babe, never got her license.

She was ninety-four when she died in 2002. She had a drawer, too, drawers and drawers of Things of Significance I fingered sacredly, brooches and costume jewelry, stretched out nylon stockings, embroidered pillowcases, rosaries, a whole drawer of twist ties and rubber bands and the backs of used envelopes. I touched everything. It was all odd and otherworldly, important because it was hers.

Only after her death did the genealogical records surface to confirm it, yes, Anna B., "born on boat." Anna B.'s mother had two other young children with her and her husband when they set sail. Her parents' names were anglicized from Stephanus and Bronislawa to Berdie and Steve. Berdie set out for a new country *that* pregnant. Berdie had already lost two infants in Slovakia. Berdie would lose two more children, ages six and age eight, in the New Country, the country of foreign tongues, the country of promise.

Berdie birthed a baby between two continents.

Ordinary Time

I can feel the heat of reverence in my fingertips still, decades removed from my mom's top dresser drawer, where she kept her Things of Significance. I open my own top dresser drawer. There's a Westminster Abbey bulletin, a map guide to Paris, ticket stubs from my trip back to the Continent, countries maybe Stephanus and Bronislawa traveled through to get my in utero great-grandmother here, to get her only son born, to get her granddaughter, to get to me. There are hospital wristbands identifying my three birthed children who survived in sterile rooms with gloved surgeons and nurses, the ones that made it despite the four we lost to miscarriage.

It is my fifteen-year-old daughter who holds in her hand the string of pearls and asks to wear them now. They make her look old, too old, too much like a woman who came before her. *Someday these things will be yours to wear, yours to bear*, I think, watching her in the mirror. I unlatch the strand and put it back in the drawer.

You can tell they're real because of the knots, I hear my great-grandmother say, showing me the way we're strung together.

Ordinary Time

The marketing agency I work at is meeting with a local business owner in this small but increasingly optimistic Rust Belt town. We talk about packaging. They make corrugated boxes. We say we're here to help them dream bigger dreams, but mostly they're looking for a shinier website and a way to get a call from some new customers. The meeting runs pretty much to script—what does success look like? Who is the hero of your story? What is the process for doing business with you? What is the call to action?

I want to show them how the folding cardboard box they manufacture is printed with artwork designed to tell how the medicine inside will help soothe the frantic mother's newborn son's fever so they can both sleep tonight and skip the unnecessary emergency room visit.

See how much this box matters? What you do matters so much! That's nice, these stories, but they really want to know the ROI. How's my SEO? What's the CTR? How much time and money is it going to take?

In the course of six months, I've worked with four different packaging companies, all within an easy drive of my office, all of which do things just a little bit differently. They aren't competitors. They manufacture corrugated boxes and display cases and windowed packages. We talk about polybags, shrink film, and bubble wrap. We talk about Contact Us forms and product menus. We talk about assembly lines and shipping and why they are the superior corrugated box manufacturer in the Midwest.

I set my limit at five of these sorts of meetings a week because they take so much time. Sometimes that's what we hit and other times there are fewer.

Everything made had to be made.

Ordinary Time

This is an ordinary time in my life. In the liturgical calendar, Ordinary Time stretches long between the last days of Eastertide until the start of Advent. It's the season in which nothing much happens. Jesus just walks around and teaches his disciples, heals a few people, holds a few dinners for sinners and tax collectors. The Israelites just wander around a while in a desert eating something fluffy and trusting God will make a more dramatic move, again, perhaps tomorrow, perhaps next year, maybe someday forty years from now.

I work forty hours a week writing marketing plans and leading strategy sessions for local business owners. We start off with a Monday team meeting in which we pray for friends and customers, share something positive, and give an update on the week ahead. On Wednesdays we have a leadership team meeting and sometimes a team lunch with whoever's available.

In the time wrapped around work, my children rise and obey their teachers, mostly. My husband and I are past the days of babies being born, still five years from our oldest leaving the house. We feed them breakfast and dinner and pay for their school lunches. After work, my husband and I walk the same loop every evening so the dog will poop in the unoccupied grassy space between the road and the soccer field. Tonight we might drink bourbon instead of wine, watch *Friends* instead of *The Office*.

I turn forty in three years and my husband is forty-two. We're at the middlest middle of our middle-income, Midwest life.

※

One of our clients owns a number of nursing homes—or to be more politically correct, senior living communities. The primary target audience is the son or daughter, usually the daughter, tasked with finding a solution for an elderly parent, the parent who is normally stubborn and unwilling to consider the need for a change. During our kickoff meeting, I bring up the constant strain, the dread of something happening, the guilt of failing your parent, the need for necessities to be met so you can enjoy the time you have left with them.

On the way to work, my mom and I talk on the phone about her mom. My mom is the primary target audience for this customer of mine. We run laps around the same impossible solution to the problem of an elderly parent living alone. We talk on the phone nearly every morning on the way to work. It's a short commute, but we cover a lot of distance—all the doctor's appointments, Dad's latest thoughts about retirement, plans for traveling, her own precarious health and all the mundane details of my life, my relationship with my husband, what's new with my kids.

While I keep trudging along in Ordinary Time, my mom is living in Lent, or maybe Holy Week, maybe even Maundy Thursday. She is living each day in the shadow of her terminal illness. Every moment is lined with this reality: death has already called ahead and made his reservation.

Living in a small town, I often interact with clients who are also friends, who also attend church with my family, who also listen with us to live bands at the local brewery on Friday night. One such friend comes in with a hospice care provider for a kickoff meeting. Even hospice has competitors edging in for business, and business is usually good when it comes to death. Someone is always dying, am I right? I try to take a more humorous approach in a short video ad I script and know even as I laugh that this is not going to fly. I send the brief marketing video to my friend anyway, knowing she'll smile, knowing she wishes we could make death a laughing matter.

In our meeting with the local hospice care provider I think about my mother. I think about the numbered days until her body loses its fight against the rebel cells it made in her kidneys and lungs and lymph nodes. And because it's two in the afternoon in the large meeting room and I am not alone in the middle of the night awake with my worst fears, I think about what it would be good to see in my Facebook feed if today was the day the doctor recommended hospice care. What would I need to know? What would I need to hear? I jot down what we write on the whiteboard and nod as we discuss the best digital solutions for marketing end-of-life care.

I think about death almost every day these days. I'd prefer not to, but it doesn't seem to want to give up its grip. There are times when I am driving that my mind will flash, imagine what might happen if I just let go of the steering wheel, what would happen when my car struck against the guard rail. Sometimes when we're walking on the sidewalk and my son is riding his bike I picture his balance wobbling, him falling wrong and into the road and into the path of a speeding car, and I blink and panic and push away the way ordinary can become extraordinary in a second, just like that, just like that and everything I've written off as typical and mundane becomes scarce and precious and gone.

Ordinary Time

But for now, it is still my Ordinary Time.

Tonight, my boys are battling in a virtual world against some coded enemies they probably generated themselves, stacking technological blocks toward a career that probably doesn't even exist yet. I grow weary of the real-world battles in which I'm the enemy who limits screen time and hides the devices so they have to actually interact with me and the wild life we've given them here, tucked between a quiet college campus and a sharp sloping hillside where trees tumble toward a creek, muting the chaos of the engineered world.

"Go outside!" I screech.

When we finally wrest the iPods and iPads and Kindles from our youngest's hands, he crouches low to the earth and whispers to the toads and garter snakes in all of that wildness until they come to him from under the leaves. He collects what he finds in an aluminum tub someone must have made somewhere in a factory.

We haven't yet worked with an aluminum tub manufacturer. Besides the box guys, there are custom tool people, screw people (so many innuendos), pump people, control panel people, and people who make things whose application it takes us months to understand. They make widgedidgedoos that can be used for a whole host of things! Everyone needs a thingamajig in their whatsitdo. I bet you didn't even know it.

When the aluminum tub manufacturer comes in, I will listen to their stories. I will learn how these tubs are the most durable and solid, multipurpose tubs you can find. But what they will not know yet is how especially good aluminum tubs can be for toad habitats made by eight-year-olds.

Our youngest son is dragging his aluminum tub toad habitat through the backyard right now, whining about having to let the toads go. It is night, the end to yet another day.

Sometimes at night I catch the sunset through the pines in the valley below our home before the next episode of *The Office* begins. Its bright notes rise orange and red until the green of the trees is made black. It is getting dark and now that I've gotten the boys to go out I worry they won't come back.

"It's time to come in!" I screech.

Ordinary Time

Go outside, come back in, eat your dinner faster, why are you chewing like you're in a race? You never tell us anything. Would you three stop talking so much? Stop having fun! Why are you so serious? These are our daily efforts to manipulate time and our children to behave the way we expect them to. They need to grow up someday, so they can arrive for their ride on the carrousel, so they can be prepared . . . for what? This?

If I opened the windows tonight, I would hear the choir of crickets and frogs, the birds finding their final evening song; maybe even the owl known to nest between our house and the next might call, if I listen.

When I put the days and weeks underneath a microscope, the way my youngest studies the earth for movement in the fallen leaves, I find filaments growing, weaving, braiding, strengthening, becoming something of greater substance. If I listen, the days and weeks stop being so much the same, so monotonous with their Monday morning meetings and Wednesday morning yoga practice, Thursday afternoon kickoff session, Friday night pizza. This is the schedule, the framework for the day, not the substance of the thing. If I listen, I find life.

So much is held together, tenuous. Death for my mom, while having placed its call, is still some distance away, staved off by modern medicine. As long as grief isn't suddenly forced upon us, knocking the wind from our guts and robbing something precious from us, we straddle the length of time right smack dab in the middle, between Advent and Lent, trudging along in Ordinary Time.

Death is distant for us, the way all of the big unknowns for my husband and I are cemented in the past, the college and career and spouse and child choices, the hometown and relocation choices, all made already and resolved, so that there's so much time for us to fill with marketing work and swim practice and morning exercise and episodes of *The Office*.

Almost-forty and just-over-forty.

Forty is a number of substance for biblical scholars. It's a number that means preparation. Any time it appears in Scripture you can bet that something's happening. Forty years of wilderness for the Israelites before entering the Promised Land. Forty days of wilderness for Jesus before his encounter with the Devil. Forty days following the Resurrection of Christ to prepare the disciples for ministry.

Ordinary Time

At almost-forty and just-over-forty, we're at the midlife point commonly labeled "crisis."

But these aren't days of crisis. They are days of preparation. There's so much ordinary time to fill it feels a little full, a little empty, a little bit like wandering about, a little bit without a purpose. Shouldn't something be *happening*?

But isn't it all happening? Isn't everyone doing something to make something else happen, to make something into something else, to connect this need to this solution, to help to heal to comfort to care to love? We are gathering in conference rooms to bridge the gap between the hero and the guide, the need and the solution, the pain point and the remedy. We are gathering in rooms to connect with other humans in this small town where we'll run into each other at the bar, at church, at baby showers, at someone else's calling hours, and we'll be present in their Advent, and we'll be present in their Lent.

It's all this Ordinary Time that allows the bones to grow, because it takes rest, you know? It takes time and stillness, habit, a solid night's sleep for all the neurons to rewire and restore and recycle the day's memories. When nothing tragic or ecstatic is happening there's a lot of time spent remembering. There's a lot of time spent making meals and taking walks and taking steps that inch you ever closer, prepare you ever so slightly more for the call, the trip, the fall, the shift, the whirling frenzy, the sudden holy slip into silence, the rising.

You won't need to remember each sunrise or sunset, every Monday morning meeting, the variations in sun salutation routines your yoga instructor has led you through these past nine months of regular practice—but isn't the way you breathe different now, isn't it good, how someone Monday will pray, someone will praise, someone will be grateful. Isn't it lovely the way the pine trees looked last night against the red of the sky, the wispy way the smoke from a neighbor's fire weaved its way into the atmosphere and disappeared, the way wood morphs into flame and ash into dust, the way the flicker hypnotizes and stirs, the way we were moved, if only this one small inch closer?

Little Joys: Walkability

WHEN we bought our home, we didn't consider what has become one of its many highlights: walkability. If you draw a circle with a one-mile radius around our house, everything I need on a regular basis lands within that mile. Our kids' schools. Two parks. The entire Ashland downtown. Three coffee shops. Our church. The university. A hospital. Our dentist *and* our orthodontist. If you edge the circle out just a teensy bit further, I could even walk to my doctor's office if need be.

There are financial benefits to this proximity, but I've also discovered mental, emotional, physical, and spiritual benefits. These days, I share a car with my daughter, who drives far more than I need to, so if I have a coffee date, or if I have a meeting with someone, or if I want to go to yoga, or whatever, 90 percent of the time, I can walk where I need to go.

Walking changes the rate at which your brain processes things. When I walk, I notice the changing colors of the grass as the seasons turn over. I notice squirrels scurrying up trees. I notice flowers growing where flowers ought not to find space to grow. I notice the changing of trees, the steady progress of construction, the rate my heart is beating, the strain of the muscles I've neglected, the speed of the clouds, the earth's gradual tilting away from the sun, the gradual tilting back toward the light and how that impacts the morning and afternoon sky, the places the sun appears, the way the rays break through.

I notice (and even acknowledge) other people. When you walk somewhere, there's a chance you will run into someone else who's walking, too, a run-in and catch-up conversation that would never have happened if you both were busy speeding to your destination.

Ordinary Time

I never have to find a place to park when I walk. I generate no exhaust when I walk. I don't have to pay for gas when I walk.

I can walk with no destination in mind, or walk for the sheer joy of going somewhere. You can't rush when you're walking—if you do, you'll show up wherever sweaty and hot and out of breath, and besides all of that, how much quicker can you get there, really, if you're jogging compared to walking?

Walking gives me a different perspective on my neighborhood and my community, an intimacy I miss if I'm driving.

This casual, steady, meandering stroll from point A to B and back home again is just one of many secret treasures our community holds, a gift that can feel like a curse or a blessing, depending on the moment, depending on the hurry or fuss or season or patience or pace of life required.

But most days, these days, I love walking.

The Things We've Lost and Where They're Found

February 2021

THE pancake batter bowl is missing.

I have twice opened and shut every kitchen cabinet drawer it could have been stuffed into by one of three children annoyed by the daily chore of unloading the dishwasher: *grooooan*. Maybe it was the jesterly husband with all his high-minded opinions about where and how certain dishes ought to be stacked. Perhaps an unaware parent, eager to help but unsure where her grown daughter stores such vessels, placed it in the most unlikely place.

Why is the place they think makes the most sense to store things never where I would have stashed them? I've even searched the other realms where our children hide things: bathroom vanities, the basement sink, the "Man Cave" where all the empty snack bags and candy wrappers congregate.

I have asked all three children and, wouldn't you know it, none of them know the whereabouts of the pancake batter bowl. It has gone the way of other things that have disappeared this year: the lid to my husband's travel mug, cookie cutters, the KitchenAid mixer bowl, one of four African dwarf frogs from our fish tank, the functionality of my autonomic nervous system, forty-five other halves to unmatched socks, the 872 words and actors and movie titles I've misplaced—enough bits to make a villanelle to rival Elizabeth Bishop.

Add it to the long line of leavers this year, the grandparents and songwriters and lovers, the lost jobs and lost businesses and lost health and lost dogs and lost balance, everything Lost now huddling somewhere together safely and sadly but soundly in the Found.

One of them is hiding my pancake batter bowl, I just know it.

There are other bowls, of course, stainless steel and glass in various sizes and depths, but this one had a handle and spout. It had a flat bottom perfect for mashing bananas with a potato masher, perfect for every Saturday banana pancake morning, perfect for pouring onto the electric griddle where the batter sizzled and bubbled and popped in its puddle of melted butter. It's what we hoped to do this morning, my youngest son and I, *make the banana pancakes, pretend like it's the weekend now,* Jack Johnson style.

We must make do with a lesser container. The metal of the masher smacks against the curved edge and misses large chunks of banana. My youngest son cracks the eggs and begins whisking the batter while the griddle warms. He doesn't seem to understand my distress. While he whisks, once more, I open and shut the cabinet drawers I've already checked. He is nine. The last ten months of remote learning have been divine hours spent home with Mom and Minecraft, making banana pancakes and pretending like it's the weekend just about every day. We pray and hug and ritually kiss forehead then chin then cheek then cheek then nose then lips each night. He prays for the virus to go away, prays for the vaccine to come, prays his mom will feel better, prays the sick people will be healed, prays the leaders would just listen for once, prays for friends and children of Lost ones to be comforted.

It is cruel, the way so much has been stolen, whether snatched from us or trashed, or abandoned in the fort the kids built in the woods (I still suspect the conniving wide-eyed convicts who live here), so much just simply and profoundly lost no one in all this remote and distanced space can find the space to make sense of it. The writers send perilous tweets and private messages, abandon hopes of narrative. The artists paint faces with missing appendages. The satellite news commentators fill the screen with ticker tape and numbers I fear will start turning over as I watch, like an old-fashioned trip odometer, turning over in real time like the real-time loss that's actually happening instead of the quiet, sad update a graphics coordinator must do during commercial breaks.

I search my bookshelf for answers but come up short on titles I must have lent to friends; this one you must read, I said, missives of hope and light packed tight between paperback covers. These ones aren't lost but borrowed, perhaps passed on and dog-eared, each one a little gospel I've sent and preached as powerful against the darkness. I finished one such book today by Brian Doyle, a writer lost to cancer, the posthumous work *One Long River of Song* aptly subtitled, *Notes on Wonder*.

"Lost," something one gets inside these pages. "Lost," somewhere one finds oneself again.

"I think I am a miracle," my youngest son says, while whisking the eggs and banana and vanilla and peanut butter that will turn from frothy liquid into solid, flat, and flippable cakes we'll smother in maple syrup in a minute. "I think I'm a miracle, because when I give you Henry hugs I make you feel better."

All, it turns out, is not lost.

I have lost the pancake batter bowl, or the pancake batter bowl was taken, or the pancake batter bowl is stashed in the most unreasonable place and will turn up again someday, after it's been replaced, the interior scratched from these last seventeen years of being beaten for pancake batter. It will limp up the front walk with a crutch under its one handle. It will have that look in its eye, that look that knows nothing can ever be again as it once was, but at least it's home. At least it's home.

The Wonders of Massaman Curry

We ate massaman curry for the first time eight or nine years ago at Rice Paper, an unassuming Thai restaurant tucked between The UPS Store and a cell phone repair place in the middle of a strip mall. No one would have known it was so good without a solid recommendation, which we had from our folks. Isn't that how it goes with most ethnic food restaurants in the Midwest, pocketed in the worn-out blue jeans of tired Rust Belt economies?

Brandon and I had whisked away our friends Steve and Angie for a kid-free night. We didn't know what to order, so we ordered some of everything—the red curry, the yellow curry, the green curry, and the massaman—and we split a bottle of wine and tried at least three appetizers, too, because our children were small, and not there.

Every appetizer and curry was moanfully delicious, and we *mmmmed* throughout our meal, laughed and asked after each other's children, shared our children's activities and idiosyncrasies and charms, and wondered, would there be more children? They had the one, so far, having started later than us. We already had three children. We had been the young and eager couple with babies always on the way, always in tow, always in need of a nap or a diaper or a meal. I had been pregnant and then not pregnant and then pregnant and then not pregnant, birthing and losing babies for over a decade.

We had taken our youngest, Henry, to his first Cleveland Indians game as a four-week-old and met Steve behind the third-base line. Henry wore a Tribe onesie, and I wrapped him in a blanket with Chief Wahoo stitched in the corner. Angie was supposed to go, too, but she had recently

The Wonders of Massaman Curry

miscarried. My four-week-old son's existence, after two live births and four miscarriages—the wonder of it—pulsed brightly in my arms.

At Rice Paper, all that miscarriage grief was gone, or buried, or scarred over, and we had new challenges: babies and aging and clock-ticking challenges. My clock had decidedly stopped with Henry because of the previous two C-sections and four miscarriages. He would be our last. We knew it before he was even conceived. If he had not become, there would have only been two, just two.

Time was short and the night was young, so after dinner we took our friends to a local tavern, where we continued our separately gendered conversations, Brandon and Steve talking about sports, probably, and Angie and I talking about books and faith and children and our husbands. I likely bemoaned the long fall football season and its road trips and its drinking and its impatient, irate husband. (It's what I did back then.) She shared how her mother-in-law, Martha, told her there were long years where she didn't really like her husband much. She still loved him, but she didn't really like him. I nodded, yes.

Martha and her husband Dan were the couple we thought of when we thought of couples we wanted to be like when we grew up. They danced and laughed and sang at our wedding. We could be that couple, someday.

In that moment on our barstools, Brandon and I in our separate conversations, so very much in love with each other but still not sure whether we would make it past this hard season, I could understand love but not like. I could laugh and sing and hold hands with Brandon, talk and drink and eat with Angie and Steve, and keep these two truths together, feel their weight, and wonder what would happen next.

Wonder is the emotion we feel that spurs us on to learn more. Cousin to curiosity, it drives the pursuit of planets in other universes, the quest for quarks inside atoms inside cells inside humans and everything in between. Humans are ever on the pursuit of something, driven by the wonder that it could all actually be at all, and how, and why. Wonder is a seed of empathy, the sunlight that makes compassion grow and change your heart into a fuller, larger person, more complete, more whole, more aware of what others need outside of your own small wants and desires.

Ordinary Time

I found the massaman curry recipe on Pinterest because we lived far enough away from Rice Paper now to make it impractical to eat good Thai food more than once in a long while, and I liked the challenge of cooking something other than what my ethnicity passed down to me. I could make chicken and rice. I could make chili. But I wondered: Could I make massaman curry? Did I have it in me to make massaman curry?

In the list of the world's fifty most delicious foods, massaman curry ranked number one in the CNNGo 2011 and 2018 reports. The dish has Muslim roots, its name a hop, skip, and a jump from the archaic Persian word for "Muslim," *mosalman*. This fact may have caused me to shrink away from Thai cuisine when I was a younger Christian, afraid of everything, the way I shrunk away from yoga (the demons!). I wasn't raised with a foreign palate, and I ingested the prejudices of my predecessors, still hear the echoes of labels that were slapped on every single Other as I grew up. I have to fight them back when the neurons in my mind are triggered and I remember the slurs, the mockery, the hate. The mind is the most complex structure in the universe, each of us a kingdom of pipes and programming and reason and irrationality. Reconfiguring its systems takes work. Disentangling baseless fear takes time and effort. Filling the mind's empty places with love takes intentionality and prayer.

Over time, the walls of my mind's kingdom have gotten lower and lower, so low now that some people feel I have abandoned biblical truth. I'm not yet sure what they mean since the truth I find in the Bible keeps reiterating through all the text's complexity the most important things: Love. Be merciful. Have compassion. But this is too simple, too watered down, not just enough. That's fine, I think to myself, massaman curry is so good, and real, and true, and beautiful, it must be made of the ingredients of God, just like every other good and real and true and beautiful thing, stitched together by the divine.

Speaking of openness and forgiveness and the largeness of God's love, I led a Sabbath study at church just this morning in the middle of a migraine episode. This week's lesson from Walter Brueggemann was on Sabbath as resistance to exclusivism:

> The community welcomes members of any race or nation, any gender or social condition, so long as that person is defined by justice, mercy, and compassion, and not competition, achievement,

production, or acquisition. There is no mention of purity, only work stoppage with a neighborly pause for humanness.[1]

There are no barriers to entering into God's community, and yet all around are measuring sticks and ticket collectors, bouncers at the doors checking to see if you're wearing the right wristband. It is the Sabbath today, and I am making massaman curry, a Muslim dish, wondering about God's Kingdom and bigger tables.

What I want is to fill all my days with Sabbath so that there might always be space for "a neighborly pause for humanness"—space for more awe, more wonder, more love for the other.

All of these flavors melding is a divine act of celebration. Massaman curry became what it is through 17th century foreign trade routes: spices moving from the Middle East through India to reach Thailand, where they combined with native flavors and local produce to produce this unique dish I found on Pinterest and made on another continent, in the Midwest-est part of the Midwest, where we make mostly steak and potatoes, in the year of our Lord 2022. Oh, wonder of wonders, how we're all here together. The world is larger and smaller than we've ever known, more interconnected, planet and atom, quark and stardust, Imago Dei in everything, swirling among our many spices and flavors.

So let there be massaman curry.

※

I stewed the chicken in the clear coconut milk that had separated in the can, and I boiled the potatoes, then whisked the red curry paste with the creamy coconut milk remains in my red French oven, then added in bay leaf, brown sugar, Worcestershire sauce, lime juice, a pinch of cinnamon, and a few shakes of cayenne pepper to give it extra kick.

It's been a quiet Sunday, one that began with a migraine and ended with us around the table, Brandon and me and two of our three children (the other at a church event). One child wanted the curry and the other settled for leftovers.

There was a time I would make them eat what I made, even if there were other options, make them sit and pout and grimace and gag and sometimes even cry before I succumbed, *Fine! Eat something else!* But these days I try to remember that food is for the nourishment of our bodies and

1. Brueggemann, *Sabbath as Resistance*, 55.

our souls, and requiring obedience to my authoritarian parenting when there are other options in the fridge to help them make it to the next meal is to create guilt and shame, contrary to the freedom I profess in Christ. I want food to mean communion, a love feast not a torture fest. Eat, eat, eat whatever you like, so long as it fills you up and helps you grow. So, my son Elvis ate leftovers. Henry, who is ten now, finished his curry first.

"This curry is delicious," Brandon said as we finished eating. There's just enough heat from crushed red pepper that we had to lean in for a long kiss of cool water on our tongues and lips.

I have it in me to make massaman curry.

※

As I cooked, I also chased around our new puppy while Brandon watched football in the other room.

"Could you monitor the dogs so they don't eat each other's food?" I called from the kitchen, my vegetables and chicken bobbing in the curry, simmering.

"What? I'm watching the AFC Championship football game!"

"How dare I disrupt this important occasion!" I called back, and he laughed, and kept watching, and I kept chasing the dogs and stirring the pot, simmering.

But then after dinner he sent me a link to something he knew I might like and took our daughter to her church event, and then he took our middle son to youth group, and then he showed me a video of one of our friend's children who has cerebral palsy. He cannot speak but loves the Bengals so much that he laughed and moaned as they celebrated Cincinnati's win, and together Brandon and I wiped our eyes, and together we cleared the table.

Every day there seems to be something else I learn that makes me wonder what I don't yet know about this particular man I have committed to love these last eighteen years, these however many more to come. He just keeps opening up more of himself to me. Just when I think I have him figured out, there's more, more and more, an evolving, expansive delight of life unfolding and becoming right in front of me.

(Just this year, the Cleveland Indians changed their name to the Guardians, because enough people wondered whether it was okay to name a sports team after a people group that wasn't even Indian in the first place, and decided, no. Some people were sad and others angry but plenty of people agreed it was good, the right thing to do, to see a group of people as more than mascots, and probably some people will say they are going to boycott the team but really, they'll show up this season, because it's still their city and their team, which they love, even if they don't like the times, how they are a changin'.)

How fickle it is to like someone; how essential it is to love. Dan and Martha are still together. Steve and Angie are still together. Brandon and I are still together. The Cleveland Guardians will still have fans this season. Maybe we'll take our children, let them pick out their own concession stand treats, meet up with Angie and Steve and their family, dance and sing and laugh at each other's children's weddings, whoever they marry, whatever they seek to do with their marvelous, wondrous lives. Love holds space for the journey. Love makes grace for the unfolding.

Little Joys: Bodies That Can Heal

It is amazing that our bodies can heal. Is there a single object that humans have made that can mend itself when it breaks? No phone screen, computer, light bulb, or battery can just automatically fix itself when it senses something is wrong. Sure, you could install a virus protector (which is essentially an immune system for a computer), but our bodies can actually break—broken bones and torn nails and burnt skin—and through the mighty power of blood and neurons and time, they can heal themselves.

When our kids have had small scrapes or scratches that made them complain about their pain or feel sad that they'd been injured, I have often reminded them, but isn't it amazing that God made our bodies so they can heal?

I've never appreciated this more than after recovering from a chronic illness. I say "recovery" with a little hitch in my breath, because generally speaking, once you have POTS, or postural orthostatic tachycardia syndrome, you always have POTS, but sometimes your body will recover to the point of normalcy again. Also, it might take longer to recover from other illnesses with POTS, or other illnesses can trigger a POTS attack and set you back again.

All of that being said, today, I have felt myself again. When I dip down to pick up something I have dropped, I marvel that I can do that without my head spinning or without losing my balance. And instead of the little beaten soldier in charge of vocabulary having to trudge back into the folds of my brain with a flashlight and a limp in order to find the word I know I know, sometimes it just *surfaces*, there it is, the word I knew I knew and didn't even have to think so hard to find. "Eureka, you found it!" I shout with glee to my battered but recovered Captain Thesaurus, who grins with unabashed pride.

Maybe that's the best part of having journeyed through this long stretch of COVID recovery: doing things again without having to think about them. POTS is a form of dysautonomia. Dysautonomia disrupts the automatic functions your body normally does on its own. Your body was made to breathe, beat, sweat, and heat without your conscious mind doing anything about it. Your autonomic nervous system is the man behind the curtain you normally don't have to pay any attention to; he just makes Oz go.

When you can't stoop down, spin around, reach high, or stand up from bed without consciously preparing yourself for whatever might happen next (dizziness, headaches, blackouts, weakness), everything has to be done carefully.

But now, now, everything I do I can do care-freely. I can do all of those things—stoop, spin, reach, stand, and even more—and when it just happens and I don't even have to think about it, it feels like magic. *Wow*, I think to myself in wonder, *you're better. You have a body that can and has healed.* It's miraculous in the way every little thing is miraculous if you look close enough.

I say bodies that "can" heal because of course sometimes they don't, and when they don't, we're left to grapple with the finitude of all things, how all things pass away, how even the stuff of miracles eventually dies... even if it rises again. So, even if... even *if* this body doesn't heal next time, even if healing isn't physical, all things are being made new, all things are being regenerated, all atoms and elements are disconnecting and reassembling into the next new thing, and that, too, is miraculous, a whole universe of interconnected miracle.

The Resurrection Life

Mom called in the middle of my coffee date at Goldberry. I let the call go to voicemail; things were probably fine. I talk to my mom nearly every day, ever since she was first diagnosed with stage four kidney cancer seven years ago.

We live far enough apart that it's hard to get together regularly, what with my three kids and husband and job, but I always intend to see her once a week. Intentions sometimes slip away and one week becomes two, maybe three if things get really busy. Then, I remember the incurability of stage four kidney cancer, the five years or so that had been given to her seven years ago, and we make plans.

My coffee date ended. I had to write an article. Normally, I'd head home to work, but the article was short, and I still had coffee to drink, so I stayed, forgetting my mom until the phone rang again.

"Hi, Mom! How's it going?"

Most everyone knows the story of Lazarus. Mary and Martha sent word to Jesus—"The one you love is sick"—but Jesus didn't bother to rush to his friend's side until he heard the news that Lazarus died. "If You had been here," Mary sobbed, "my brother would not have died."[1] You can hear the unspoken accusation, *Where were You? Didn't You hear me? Why didn't You do something?*

---

1. John 11:1-21 (NIV).

The question we ask when things go badly tends to be, "Why me?" Sometimes when things go well, we ask that same thing.

I've found the "why me" to be useless. The times I've asked it, all it has done is whirled me into a frenzy of self-pity, anger, rage, resentment, and sadness. "Why me" has no vision except inwardly. In its attempt to make sense of the world, all it sees is the self as somehow special—either spared or damned—compared to everyone else. "Why me" makes me stare at my own guts in grief.

Why *not* me?

"Oh, I'm good. I'm just on my way home from the doctor's office. Are you sitting down?"

All the mourners thought He was crazy when Jesus asked them to roll away the stone, but Jesus only cared what His Father thought, and His Father thought that Lazarus should live—even if it seemed insane, to think a dead man could live again. Plenty of people had begged Jesus to heal their bodies. Some even thought their people were already dead, but Jesus said they were just asleep. He said to them, *get up, shake off your graveclothes.*

Some dared to expect a miracle. *I know that even now God will give you whatever you ask.*[2]

"Lazarus, come out!"[3]

Before my mother's cancer diagnosis, it never occurred to me that she might die. Oh, sure, someday, but not soon. I had taken her presence for granted. She is here. How could there be a time when she is not?

We talk about time like it's currency, like we have so many seconds tucked into a savings deposit box somewhere. Spent time. Wasting time. Bought time. Lost time. Living on borrowed time. When the bank statement arrives and the doctor says it's stage four, what we desperately want is more time.

---

2. John 11:22 (NIV).
3. John 11:43 (NIV).

But what if the miracle isn't being given more time. What if the miracle is in the revelation of our mortality? More time would be nice, but what about the time right in front of us, the time we're just spending without seeing its holiness, coasting along with no regard for the fullness of time, how each moment is charged with the miracle of *being*?

If we lean into this awareness, we fall into the pool of grace and climb out into resurrected life. We die to the old rules about time as currency, and we live with the new, that time is filled with every measure of love, waiting for us to engage it, waiting for us to celebrate the miracle of every moment, interconnected and glorious and *now*.

※

"The doctor went over my scans from last week," my mom told me. "He said the cancer is gone."

"You're kidding." I sat down. "That's amazing!" I stood up. I said, "That's unbelievable!" I paced around the small room adjacent to the main coffee shop. A college student was working on a computer with earbuds in as if the whole world hadn't just been born again. She wasn't paying attention.

Pay attention! I wanted to shout. *Everything living right now is alive!*

"This is amazing!" I couldn't stop saying it. "I never thought we would hear this news."

We talked for a few more minutes, about the unbelieving, the wonders. *This is a miracle!* We didn't believe the cancer could just go away, and here it is, the cancer went away!

"The doctor did say I'll probably have to go back on Inlyta again, someday," Mom said. "They'll do scans again at eight weeks, and then twelve, to make sure it isn't coming back. But I can stop taking it for now."

"Wow," I said. I tucked away that small reality, *someday* shoved off to the far horizon of our lives, and asked instead, "So, what now?"

※

Lazarus was one of a few people given a taste of the resurrected life before Jesus Himself died and rose again. Others were healed of paralysis. Others were freed from chains that bound them. Others were born again, dead to the life they had been living, alive to the miracle of love in front of them. When Jesus ascended into heaven, He left behind the apostles. The angels told them, "What are you standing around for? Go!"

This is just a moment to catch our breath. You will have to go back onto the cancer medication someday. Rejoice, you have been given the vision to see the fullness of time, how brief, how lasting.

What do we do now?

⁂

Mom and I said goodbye, and I set the phone down on the table. The college student continued studying, not paying attention. Goldberry is the sort of place that usually has a number of people who matter a lot to me hanging around. I walked out into the main area of the shop. No one I knew very well was there. I walked back toward my booth, at a loss for how to behave in a moment like this (*Can you believe this is happening?*), then pivoted again. Who cares if I don't know these people that well? People need to know!

"My mom's cancer is gone!" I shouted, laughing, raising my arms to the ceiling. Doug, the owner of the coffee shop who also leads worship at our church, came out to see what was going on. He gave me a hug.

"We thought she'd have five years," I sobbed into his shoulder. "It's been seven. It's gone! This is amazing! I never thought I'd hear this news."

"Praise God!" Doug said.

The baristas all stood grinning and weeping, watching me laugh and wipe my eyes and not know what to do with myself.

Not knowing what to do with myself, I said, "I guess I'll go home now." I gathered up my computer and my empty mug.

Everyone watched me leave. I got into the car, as if it was just another day.

⁂

I learned the next day that a beloved faculty member at the local university had just passed away from cancer. It had happened quickly, his turn from relatively good health to death so hard, so sudden. Some of the folks in the coffee shop were close to him. We waited to tell the news to other friends who were waiting on a report from their physician. I held my breath, then burst out with this God-news in front of people I knew had lost parents to cancer. How is it possible to celebrate this unearned gift in the face of such unearned grief?

But this happens every day. This is why Paul doesn't waste time telling his readers what to do in Romans 12:15, "Rejoice with those who rejoice;

mourn with those who mourn." You need to do both at once—sometimes on the same day—you need to make space for both of these sacred moments. I spent years lamenting my mom's diagnosis. How dare I fail to rejoice publicly in the face of this gift? How dare I rob my friends and family of the glory of Easter morning after so many years of holding space for the sorrow of Good Friday?

Good news. Bad news. What now? What now, what now, what now?

※

Maybe it seems obvious that we're all going to die. The tragedy is that we forget it. Today I am standing and rejoicing in the unbelievable miracle of this healing, but tomorrow? Will I forget the beautiful, deep time the awareness of my mom's mortality gave us and return to going through the motions?

Resurrection life stubbornly demands otherwise. It demands that we live in Christ's Light, rooted in Him, strengthened by Him, overflowing with thankfulness, living as Jesus did, fully present to what was happening around Him and in Him, seeing the image of God in everything and loving it fiercely.

How dare we return to how we lived before the great awakening.

※

Out came Lazarus.

All the family and friends gathered around must not have known what to do. Dance? Laugh? Stand up? Sit down? Hug? Jump around?

I think I have an idea.

Crickets

This is what I have observed to be good: that it is appropriate for a person to eat, to drink and to find satisfaction in their toilsome labor under the sun during the few days of life God has given them—for this is their lot.

—Ecclesiastes 5:18 NIV

After the diagnostic mammogram that indicated I need a biopsy next Tuesday, I have to get crickets. There are fifteen minutes until I have to pick up Henry, my youngest son who is ten-going-on-eleven. It's just enough time to pick up the crickets—three dozen large crickets—because Joey, Henry's bearded dragon, is over a year old, and he (or she, we aren't sure) eats large crickets now.

I've been hyperaware of my right breast all day, ever since the mammogram report yesterday—particularly the microcalcifications that will be under greater scrutiny next Tuesday. Next Tuesday is Henry's 11th birthday. When he was born, all he did was breastfeed, never a bottle, the entire first year of his life. He is pure sweetness, compassionate for all creatures, even for all manner of lizards and amphibians, and yet the death of the live crickets doesn't bother him. My right breast seems to be parading its recent diagnosis. Everyone who sees me sees my right breast being loud and proud of its microcalcifications, I just know it. The lady who bags up my crickets sees it throbbing and shouting, *I have microcalcifications!* My right breast is dying for attention.

Ordinary Time

Yesterday, my daughter's 16th birthday, gave me the baseline mammogram of my 40th year. Sixteen years ago yesterday was the first time I breastfed a baby; Lydia's hungry tug on me was almost orgasmic as we learned each other's wants and needs.

Were the microcalcifications in there then? Were they in there from the beginning, before I was born? Were they always and ever there, prescripted in my DNA passed down through my mom from her mom who has had her own turn with breast cancer, twice now (or maybe three times), and will that be the story I inherit, the story I've already tucked into Lydia's own DNA? My daughter who wants to get her license to take one more big step away from me, but she can't, really, no matter how far she flies. We're all of us tied up in a genetic cat's cradle of precancerous potential, connected.

I turn forty in three months. To celebrate, I am giving myself the trip of a lifetime, Out West. I'm taking my boys and we're going to drive and camp, and then we're going to stay with friends, and then my husband and Lydia are going to meet us in Salt Lake City, and then we're going to drive home, and then I will turn forty. These are my plans. Before that happens, my mother-in-law is taking Lydia and me and my sister-in-law and niece to New York City. She's covering the costs—it's a trip of a lifetime. I have said so many things today that I don't normally think about, "trips of a lifetime," for one, that carry an awful lot in their letters. I asked my husband how he was doing after yesterday's news. "Terrified," he said. That's just a couple letters removed from "terrific," how it is from moment to moment, everything terrific and terrifying then terrific again.

The crickets are trying to climb the inside of the plastic bag; they are trying to climb away from certain death, to escape the pile of crickets near the rubber-banded opening of the bag. I don't know where they think they're going to go, certainly not out into my car. I'm waiting now for Henry to come out of school. Just a few more minutes. The crickets are jumping like popcorn against the plastic bag. *Let us out!* They don't know what "out" means. They don't know how destined for death they are. They leap and scurry frantically. When I get home, I have to make dinner—chicken and rice is on my meal plan; I plan everything—and probably I'll do a load of laundry, and probably I'll walk the dogs with my husband. Probably I'll make a list of everything I need to do again tomorrow and check off what I did today, and move what I didn't do today to tomorrow. I plan everything. I've put off the dogs' heartworm pills. I should do that, so they don't die. I should do all these things but I think I'll just recline instead, close my eyes. Waste my life.

It's been a month since my mom found out her stage four kidney cancer is gone . . . for now. I am holding onto all the spaces between the dots of the ellipsis because they make an ugly promise that there's more to the story. I want to say "fuck the ellipses," but I'm not that angry of a person and I know too much about ends of sentences to rage about their finality. It's fine, all fine, fine-all.

The crickets are clawing over top of each other to get nowhere except into the wide-open orifice of Joey, who will not think a second about the clawing and will swallow each one whole.

Here comes Henry. I shuffle the scampering bag of three dozen large crickets to the armrest.

"How was your day?" I ask my son.

"Good. Are these medium crickets? They look like medium."

"They're large."

"They look like medium."

"They're large."

Joey used to be little and I liked him/her then, but now he/she kind of freaks me out. I was not aware of the live crickets dilemma—that he/she would eat living things I'd have to feed it—when I agreed to Joey as a birthday gift a year ago. Back then, Joey ate small crickets. Those didn't bother me as much, for some reason, even though it isn't like they *breed* them small; they're just younger. What's wrong with me? I'd rather have infant crickets consumed by my toddler bearded dragon instead of adults? Joey just keeps growing and needing to eat more mature piles of crickets, crickets that jump and scamper and chirp. He/she eats things alive.

"Make sure you put the crickets away when we get home."

※

I was most impressed, at first, with the size and perfection of my right breast, smashed as it was on the mammography film, filled with veins and blurry clouds and microcalcifications, my breast a diamond mine. Aww, look at you, bearer of life, all big and full like it's time to feed the infants again. Everything from the beginning of my three children's lives I carry around in my bosom. Tucked here are screams and near-death experiences, vacations and laughter, a cluster of a billion little joys (I've been singing that song today, "Little Joys," by Tom Rosenthal).

These mysterious microcalcifications are just grains of sand from the beach last month. These are just flakes of salt from the ocean, tears, the dinners I've prepared—just too much salt maybe. Cut it out (I mean the salt, cut out the salt from the diet) and boom, they'll be gone. An initial mining tap will determine their essence next Tuesday, so soon we will know—calcium, sand, diamond, salt, a stubborn cluster of little joys I've held too closely, or maybe something else.

The radiologist said that microcalcifications are most often benign nothings that have always been and always will be, but sometimes they aren't. Like 15 percent of the time or 40 percent or something, I don't know—it all depends on which site you google and how optimistic you're feeling. I don't believe in statistics and I don't believe in weighted scales or karma or coincidence or providential punishment, I don't believe in penal substitutionary atonement or getting what's coming to you, and I don't believe that God traded my mom's cancer for my budding microcalcifications, nor that He'll make that trade back again, although that's what my mom prayed last night all night. I tuck that one deep down next to the ellipsis, behind the cluster of little joys. It throbs.

I don't believe any of it. My doctrinal statement of things I believe keeps shrinking, wearing all the things of this world down to just one or two things I think I know, one or two things, maybe three, that I hope are true—faith and hope and love, but love is the last and best and final thing I have faith and hope will remain. Everything else just scampers and jumps and chirps, and then is consumed.

Statistics are not part of my doctrinal statement of things I believe. There was some ridiculous one-in-a-million chance I'd have a weird pregnancy I can't remember the name of, oh wait there it is, partial mole pregnancy, and that happened. There was a ridiculous similar statistic that my second child, my full-term infant, would have respiratory distress syndrome and that happened. My mom's cancer wasn't supposed to just go away and that happened. It just happens. It all just happens.

As a result of statistics, I don't really entertain "why me" questions; instead, I just keep singing "Why Not Me" by The Judds in my head all day long. Okay, so four things in my doctrinal statement of belief—faith, hope, love, and music. Naomi Judd just died this week of mental illness, so *why not me when the nights get cold, why not me when you're growing old, why not me.*

Crickets

It is probably fine, probably nothing, but there's another statistical word, probability, and people defy odds all the freaking time, odds are you won't die yet—*odds are that we will probably be alright,* that's another song, that one's by the Barenaked Ladies. We saw them play once, twice, maybe three times. It sucks when you beat the odds the wrong way. That keeps happening to people I love, too.

This morning I woke up with Sara Groves' song "It's Gonna Be Alright," which is more optimistic than BNL because she's a Christian artist, and she has a new hope that drops the odds and probablys to just come right out and say that it's gonna be alright. It's going to be fine. I have a new hope, too, so I sang that one a while today before the diagnostic mammogram, then remembered my favorite saint of the mystical, Julian of Norwich, and her 14th century declaration (maybe it's the summation of my doctrinal statement) that *all shall be well, all shall be well, all manner of thing shall be well.* I love its eternity-ness but hate it a little also, because a woman in my MFA program loved it and died of cancer right in the middle of her course sequence, halfway through the MFA program. She wrote beautiful poems and believed "all the right ways" (like that's a thing) and still died. And that makes me bitter for the bullshit about the good dying young—another song—and the notion that God takes people early for angelic usage, which is the most twisted, selfish thing I can think of God doing next to creating an eternal lake of fire for the people who just never had a proper introduction to Him. I'm so over that understanding of God, of anyone make-believing they have any understanding of God. There's another thing for my doctrine of things I don't believe.

I know *all shall be well,* but there's still the bag of crickets, scurrying, waiting.

I decided to let the laundry and dinner be and just recline for a minute and write this, but Ruby and Izzy, our Westies, insist on the tennis ball. *Here it is! Bark! Throw it!* Scamper scamper scamper. *Here it is! Bark! Throw it!* I throw it and throw it and throw it and they fetch it and Ruby barks and I want to destroy her. Everything feels urgent and pointless. Ruby is completely insensitive to everything I am saying but especially "STOP BARKING YOU MORON," which she keeps doing while wheeling just out of my reach. She's the puppy, a hyper, adolescent puppy who thinks only of her own needs and is constantly telling us about them except when she has to pee, and then she just does it. She lets you hold her like a baby, like a baby against your chest, and rests her head on your shoulder, and then nips at your nose, *I love you.* She thinks biting our noses is a kiss because she's seen Henry give us goodnight kisses, and that's as close as she can get to smacking her lips. That's something I love, something else to tuck into that cluster.

While Ruby barks and barks with her ball at my feet, Izzy, the elder, sits on my lap and leans her snout against my chest, against the right breast where all my microcalcifications nest with the little joys, holding all their potential. We got Ruby to offset the future potential sadness of losing Izzy. Like that's going to work. Izzy looks into my eyes and knows. *All shall be well*, her big watery eyes of God say to me. *Let's take a walk. Let's get Dad and take a walk. And when we come back,* lick smooch with that cool wet nose, *you can throw me the ball. Look at me wag my tail. I love you so much.*

All shall be well. All manner of thing. *It's gonna be.* Why not me? Little joys of the finite.

I go to check, and sure enough, when we got home, Henry transferred the crickets from the plastic bag to their new abode. They're content now. They sit and eat the gritty cricket food, drink water from a dampened paper towel, merry in the freedom from the plastic bag, oblivious to the gradual disappearance of their neighbors, taken up through the open door one by one. Joey hears their scratching from his small terrarium and waits.

What Did and Didn't Last

It's been twenty years since you undid the bobby pins from my updo, twenty years since we said a couple I Do's to promises we couldn't really keep yet—for worse, for poorer, in sickness, till death—all in faith that everything we had right then would last. But packaged back in our rental house on Leland Avenue were boxes and boxes of products that wouldn't make it to see this anniversary.

What is still here—the good soup ladle, pasta spoon, and metal spatula (but not the junk we got at the Dollar Store, of course), half the silverware, most of the steak knives, the electric griddle (so many pancake Saturdays, so many bananas, so many chocolate chips, gallons of maple syrup), the pasta strainer but none of the wheat pasta. Not the Foreman grill. The KitchenAid mixer, but not the pancake batter bowl.

Our entire first (and second, and third) set of plates, bowls, and mugs is long gone, dropped and chipped and cracked from Akron to Ashland and back again, twice. We've lost two of the fancy crystal wine goblets and one of the little crystal liqueur glasses, but all of the multicolored champagne flutes remain (our three kids like to sip their bubbly grape juice from them and then leave them out for someone else to wash, like they're at a fancy party, don't worry, the help will take care of them).

Between Leland and Berry Avenues, we've left behind four houses, three dogs, several fish, and a bearded dragon named Joey, lost four babies and several visions of what our future would look like, and I think we finally got rid of all of those identical T-shirts you had in a box when we first moved in. The slow fashion, spaghetti jars as cups, Recyclops, compost queen in me now wonders what I was thinking?! We could have saved so much money and landfill square footage if I had just let you keep wearing that exact same shirt for the last 240 months!

We walked around Target in the in-between engagement and wedding days armed with a laser scanner and ideas about what it would take to make our new home. You scanned the most ridiculous things, just to see what people might buy for us. I picked what seemed affordable, practical, and reasonable. You chose a flat-screen TV, which was absurd because no one had those back then and no one was going to buy that for us; I couldn't believe you registered for that, would you stop it! I had to keep taking the radar gun from your grip and deleting the ridiculous from our list.

My one aunt ignored my Teflon pots and pans and went off-script, buying us the nicest set of KitchenAid pots and pans we didn't register for, which was just like her. They're still here, along with the ridiculousness that ignites each day with you, laughter punctuating our daily dance in a kitchen I never dreamed of in a life beyond our imagination with three children further apart from each other than the points of the largest triangle and yet somehow just like us in a million different ways, all filled with your ridiculousness and maybe some of my stubborn practicality, and our grins as we torment them with unabashed affection as our two, twelve-pound white devil angels demand to be walked and fed and loved in this town we didn't imagine moving to or returning to or staying in with all these people whose lives have become inextricably entwined with ours. We even still have some fish that won't die.

I would take it all again: the thumbs that didn't last, the jobs that didn't last, the health that didn't last, the valley and mountaintop seasons that didn't last, the million major and minor deaths we've borne witness to these last twenty years. I would take it all again for the life that keeps being resurrected here, each day, the life that keeps evolving into new guitars and dishwashers, fresh pillows and better sheets, plates that don't break, the lesson they are teaching me that if you invest in something good, it just might last.

Bibliography

Brueggemann, Walter. *Sabbath as Resistance: Saying No to the Culture of Now.* Louisville: Westminster John Knox, 2014.

Doyle, Brian. "Mister Louie." In *Leaping: Revelations and Epiphanies,* 52. Chicago: Loyola, 2003.

Donne, John. "No Man Is an Island." All Poetry, accessed January 3, 2024, https://allpoetry.com/No-man-is-an-island.

Hanna, Jason, et al. "Alleged shooter at Texas high school spared people he liked, court document says." *CNN,* May 18, 2018, https://www.cnn.com/2018/05/18/us/texas-school-shooting/index.html.

McKelvey, Douglas. "A Liturgy for the Preparation of a Meal." In *Every Moment Holy, Volume 1.* Nashville: Rabbit Room, 2017.

WebMD. "Ortho Tri-Cyclen Oral: Uses, Side Effects, Interactions." Accessed January 8, 2024, https://www.webmd.com/drugs/2/drug-17131/ortho-tri-cyclen-28-oral/details.

www.ingramcontent.com/pod-product-compliance
Lightning Source LLC
Chambersburg PA
CBHW071206160426
43196CB00011B/2206